# DESIGNERS
# AT HOME

# DESIGNERS AT HOME

## PERSONAL REFLECTIONS
## ON STYLISH LIVING

### RONDA RICE CARMAN
#### FOREWORD BY MARTHA STEWART

*RIZZOLI*
NEW YORK

New York  Paris  London  Milan

For Mason, always follow your dreams.

In memory of Amy Richards,
Elizabeth Becker, and Michael Schmidt—
you each lived life stylishly.

First published in the United States of America in 2013 by

Rizzoli International Publications, Inc.
300 Park Avenue South
New York, New York 10010
www.rizzoliusa.com

Text © 2013 by Ronda Rice Carman

Every effort has been made to trace copyright holders of material in this book.

2013 2014 2015 2016 / 10 9 8 7 6 5 4 3 2

Printed in China

ISBN 13: 978-0-8478-4009-0

Library of Congress Control Number: 2012954523

Project Editor: Sandra Gilbert
Design by Doug Turshen with Steve Turner

# CONTENTS

# FOREWORD

There are very few subjects that don't kindle some sort of "I have to know more about that" spirit in me. Having met and worked with many, many interior designers, I have always been interested in how they, as a professional group, live their own private lives, away from their 24/7 obsessions with fabric, furniture, paintings, mirrors, rugs, and objets d'art. In this impressive volume, Ronda Carman has opened many doors into the spaces all of us want to see but often never have the opportunity to do so. Fifty well-known, highly respected designers allowed her inquisitive reporter's eye into their personal homes so we could experience firsthand just what "personal style" means to this group, and whether, to them, "home" is a sacred place for seeking comfort and refuge—a haven to escape the accoutrements of the trade—or a place to try out new ideas as a laboratory of experimentation and trial and error. The answers are many and varied and the book satisfies a lot of our questions, but it also encourages us to ask even more: What's the secret of organizing? What kind of towels does she use in the bathrooms? What kinds of hangers are in the closets?

The designers interviewed for this book have so many diverse ideas on the subject of living, and, as we study picture after picture in this veritable feast of homes, the photographs and essays make it easy for us to understand their individual philosophies and styles. The author includes excellent imagery from both inside and outside the designers' homes so we can see how exterior and interior spaces are integrated, how greenery plays an important part in so many interiors, and how, not surprisingly, designers pay close attention to the minutest details. I consider this volume a "look, study, learn" book that is neither skimpy nor superficial, but generous and informative.

Martha Stewart
New York City, 2012

# STYLISH LIVING AT HOME

I have always been a seeker of information and a collector of ideas. I love being left alone to dream and read. During the long, lazy days of summer, my mother would drop me off at the local library for a regular rendezvous with Julia Child, F. Scott Fitzgerald, and Truman Capote. For as long as I can remember, it has been my habit to amass books and as many lifestyle and fashion magazines as possible. Even at the age of twelve I devoured them. As a teen, I spent hours sitting on my bed with a notebook and pen, writing every tip and noteworthy suggestion I could gather. Some ideas were a success while others drove my mother crazy. I learned quickly that half a jar of mayonnaise is not the best hair conditioner. But I was on a quest. I wanted to know the correct way to organize my sock drawer, properly hang trousers, and do things in a better manner.

As I approached my twenties, I became obsessed with home interiors and shelter magazines, always eager to learn more from the experts. On the evening of my engagement, my soon-to-be mother-in-law presented me with a gift that forever changed my thoughts on home and entertaining: a large, tattered book and handwritten note that read, "This book brought much pleasure in my early years of marriage." That evening I climbed into bed with Dorothy Rodgers's *My Favorite Things: A Personal Guide to Decorating and Entertaining*. Two hours later I had been lured into her seductive world of cocktails, canapés, dinner parties, and parlor games. I was hooked and wanted to learn more about the intricacies of creating a beautiful home and what made interiors so inviting. My salvation came in the form of Martha Stewart's lavishly illustrated book *Entertaining*. Once again, I was instantly seduced and transported to another wonderful world. Fascinated by the engaging blonde hostess, I, too, wanted to serve cold borscht in pretty goblets, learn a better way to set the table, and grow my own flowers and vegetables.

When we moved to Scotland in 2005, all of my books, clipped articles, and hundreds of magazines came along too. It did not take long to see that my growing collection would not fit in our hundred-year-old flat, given the shortage of closet space, and so began *All the Best Blog*. After penning my first few blog posts, I knew that my tagline, *Passport to Stylish Living*, would play a pivotal role in formulating both the direction of my blog and posts.

I would venture to guess that the notion of stylish living is a topic of great fascination to many, in part because style is a concept that cannot be precisely defined, and yet we know it when we see it. I have long wondered what inspires one person to elevate the mundane tasks of daily living and another to despise the regular routines of life. In an age of increasing mass production and a recurring sea of sameness, I hold in high regard those who ponder the idiosyncrasies of living life in a unique, meaningful, and deliberate manner. To be sure, there is no one quality that defines style or a stylish existence, but it is easily recognized.

Diana Vreeland once wrote that few things are more fascinating than the opportunity to see how people live during their private hours. I agree. But for me it is more than just peering behind the door of a home that I find alluring. It is the opportunity to learn and to be witness to a myriad of ideas but most importantly to gain inspiration. As David Hicks wrote in his daughter India's autograph book, "Good taste is by no means dependent upon money." David's thoughts are a common theme in this book. Often it's the little details that make the biggest difference in our day-to-day life. Designer Vicente Wolf counts lightly starched sheets, blooming orchids, sunshine, and a surprise snack in the refrigerator among his favorite things. For me, nothing brings my day to a relaxing end like a family dinner, a hot bath, and burning a beautiful candle.

This book is the sharing of thoughts, ideas, and resources. Over the past several years, I have been privileged to meet many brilliant and inspiring designers. Several have played an important role in my life and blog, making the selection process for this book an exceedingly difficult task. There are countless designers I would have included in a heartbeat were space not an issue. This collection features not only the old guard but also emerging talents from the Americas, the United Kingdom, and Europe.

Each day as I cited the lifestyle philosophies of those gifted individuals while writing *Designers at Home*, the French literary salon came to mind. The purpose of the salon was to gather like-minded individuals under the roof of one host to increase the knowledge of the participants. Just as salons served as sources of information, inspiration, and occasions to exchange ideas, I hope this book will serve as a hardbound, modern-day version. Perhaps there will be more volumes down the road.

Ronda Rice Carman
Glasgow, Scotland, 2012

MILLER'S
20TH CENTURY DESIGN
KELLY HOPPEN INTERIORS
HAPPY TIMES / LEE R
ASSOULINE
THE WORLD OF INTERIORS JULY 2010
THE WORLD OF INTERIORS JANUARY 2010
THE WORLD OF INTERIORS FEBRUARY 2010
THE WORLD OF INTERIORS DECEMBER 2009
THE WORLD OF INTERIORS AUGUST 2009
THE WORLD OF INTERIORS JULY 2009
THE WORLD OF INTERIORS SEPTEMBER 2009
THE BEST OF INTERIORS – 25 YEARS
THE WORLD OF INTERIORS DECEMBER 2011
THE WORLD OF INTERIORS OCTOBER 2011
THE WORLD OF INTERIORS DECEMBER 2006

# KIM ALEXANDRIUK
## STYLE IS A PHYSICAL MANIFESTATION OF OUR INTERNAL CREATIVITY.

Santa Monica's Sunset Park has been called America's last Ozzie-and-Harriet neighborhood. It is a place where young families live next door to retirees, children ride their bikes on the sidewalks to school, residents shop at the local market, and neighbors gather for block parties. Most of the homes are traditional one-story houses built in the early- and mid-twentieth century. Interior designer Kim Alexandriuk's 1929 Spanish-style hacienda is one such example. Nestled among the eclectic mix of architecture, ranging from Spanish Colonial Revival to California Craftsman, the house was built by Cecil A. Gale, a prolific developer in the area during the late 1920s through the 1940s. While the home retained much of its original integrity, it was in need of updating.

Raised in Germany and educated in Lyon in fine arts, Kim worked for the Getty Museum for two years and Michael Smith for six years before opening her own interior design firm. Kim's aesthetic is an amalgam of a number of influences, including her European heritage, reverence for architecture, and passion for travel. When she and her husband, Michael, remodeled their California abode, they set out to reinterpret the original architecture. Kim is firmly of the mindset that a home should look as though it was built over time and not dedicated to a sole period or aesthetic. To that end, the couple employed clean lines, white plaster walls, driftwood-gray cerused oak floors, and oil-rubbed bronze hardware. The result is a dwelling that is both classic and up-to-date.

A workplace was added at the rear of the property to accommodate a growing design staff, while allowing the designer to be near her young son, Niko. In both her home and office, Kim incorporated details and furnishings from several eras, weaving a rich tapestry of styles. Timeless pieces, including midcentury antiques and vintage finds, harmonize with artwork by well-known abstract artist Werner Drewes and local Mexican artist Lorenzo Rivera. The modern elements in

**DECORATIVE DETAILS** I love being surrounded by treasures from my travels and expressive paintings with strong colors. Details breathe life back into our home and allow our personalities and lifestyles to become part of the surroundings. They can recall a memory, tell a joke, or simply act as an extension of our life together. One item I will never forgo is a soft cashmere throw. When my mom visits and rocks my son to sleep, I drape a throw around her shoulders and another over my sleeping boy.

this traditional setting exude warmth and sophistication. All of the rooms and spaces are inviting, yet they embrace a sense of amusement. "My style is unbridled, inventive, and authentic. I always like to add a touch of humor, which draws people in and starts a conversation."

The atmosphere of the living quarters is light and cheerful, with an easy flow between light-drenched rooms. Large glass French doors not only let in sunshine but also expand the perceived size of the house while seamlessly connecting the backyard garden. An outdoor fireplace and ample seating provide the perfect spot for gathering and alfresco dining. "We really do work and live in every area of our home and garden."

**MAKING AN ENTRANCE** I see the facade of our house as the title of our family biography, and the entry as the prologue. What lies behind the door gives guests a sense of what is to come and a taste for who we are stylistically; this is the first opportunity to curate a sense of emotion. In our hallway, a pair of large-scale paintings and a 1940s French chair covered in the original leather welcome us home. I strive to create an ease that transcends the tough workday into a calm retreat.

**CREATURE COMFORTS** Hiking in the mountains of Santa Barbara, Malibu, and Santa Monica is always a peaceful getaway. Time with my darling son, my adorable husband, and our loving puppy is bliss. Our precious moments together fill my heart with love and joy.

**FLOWERS AND FRAGRANCES** I love Diptyque candles, especially the clean and woodsy aroma of Feu de Bois. The earthy scent reminds me of the forests in France. For the holidays, I prefer eucalyptus, fir, and pine for their deep warmth and festive fragrance. In the spring and summer, I go with the crisp, fresh scents of citrus and verbena. As for flowers, deep burgundy dahlias, yellow tulips, and pure white peonies are amazing. The deep purple of an iris is spectacular as well, especially when it begins to open.

**A BEAUTIFUL BED** A comfortable well-dressed bed is the ultimate indulgence. It is the one room where I can be incredibly selfish design-wise, and our guests' perceptions are of no concern. A somewhat firm mattress topped with a thick organic cotton mattress pad covered with crisp white Frette Egyptian cotton linens is pure luxury.

**ENTERTAINING THOUGHTS** Our home is tailor-made for indoor-outdoor living. When the French doors are thrown open from the kitchen to the garden, it feels as if there is no exterior wall. The best outdoor spaces not only embrace the landscape, but they also provide shelter, comfort, and a sense of style. I like to set a table with appetizers and drinks next to the outdoor fireplace. The children roast marshmallows while the adults enjoy my husband's amazing cocktails. Speakers pipe soft music through the space; it's the perfect setting for a warm summer evening. Of course, great food and a beautiful backdrop are important, but people are the magic ingredient.

# JORGE ALMADA AND ANNE-MARIE MIDY
## A STYLISH HOME IS ONE THAT IS ARTISTIC, COMFORTABLE, AND FUNCTIONS VERY WELL.

For husband-and-wife design team Anne-Marie Midy and Jorge Almada, creativity is a way of life that is reflected in their homes. Anne-Marie and Jorge are the founders of Casamidy, a contemporary furniture company based in picturesque San Miguel de Allende. The Mexican hilltop town, rich in tradition and blessed with skilled craftsmen, was the perfect spot for the couple to set up shop and start a family.

Home is a large, traditional dwelling located in the town's historic center. Reminiscent in feel to older neighboring houses, it was actually constructed in the 1960s. Endowed with natural light, sweeping views of the valley, and a striking neo-Gothic parish church, the house and neighborhood provide a constant source of inspiration. Anne-Marie and Jorge share a keen eye and global point of view—a reflection of their cross-cultural identity. Both born to American mothers—her father is French while his is Mexican—their unique blend of different heritages is immediately present the moment you enter their world. For the design-passionate pair, no ordinary entrance would suffice. Guests enter through double doors collaged with religious charms and crowned with a shell motif. A curved flight of steps leads to the bedrooms, where family and guests have a beautiful vista of the town.

From baroque mirrors to brightly colored metal Louis XVI armchairs and weathered Moroccan side tables, this is a highly personal residence. Soothing tones temper shots of color, and faded antiques provide a timeworn charm. In the main living area, concha-crowned bookshelves flank a white fireplace and hold treasured memorabilia and artwork by friends. Each room is an arresting mix of history and contemporary style, boasting

### FLOWERS AND FRAGRANCES
Anne-Marie loves the finely carved terra-cotta Amber Balls by L'Artisan Parfumeur. Handcrafted by mother-and-daughter artisans, no one ball is alike and each is scented with golden Orient amber. The exotic fragrance is magnified by a heated room. We both like wildflowers in the house, usually in white. With their relaxed structure, they make great candidates for cut-flower arrangements.

modern furniture and artisanal art as well as magnificent textiles. "We believe that every home or space will accept or reject certain colors," Jorge says. "It's important to study how sunlight reacts within the interiors at different times of the day," notes Anne-Marie, who studied color theory. Looking to bring in more natural light, the couple added large French picture windows to frame an outdoor courtyard. Graveled pathways, billowing trees, and a tiled table adorn the patio—a favorite spot for relaxing on a warm evening.

Moreover, Jorge and Anne-Marie's design aesthetic is heavily inspired by their surroundings, travel, and artisanal craftsmanship. The oft-used dining room is a faultless illustration. A massive, stripped nineteenth-century altar, found in a local antiques shop, is the perfect counterpoint to a Casamidy steel-clad-top table and hand-forged iron chandelier. Round mirrors that hang inside the altarpiece further reflect light and expand the space. It is this combination of contemporary handmade designs and antiques that infuse their rooms with joy.

After more than a decade in San Miguel de Allende, the family recently relocated to Brussels, to expand their business abroad, be further inspired, and provide their children with the experience of living in a European city. "We are keeping our house in Mexico," says Anne-Marie, "but for now we feel that Belgium offers a new adventure for our family and has a strong design perspective."

**DECORATIVE DETAILS** Our main living areas are accentuated with personal possessions reminiscent of family members or a special trip. Most people view them as decorative objects. Old things that possess simplicity are the most appealing to us. As we don't like clutter, striking a balance with our collection of furnishings and objects is our biggest challenge. Rarely do we look for pieces to fit in a certain spot or room, but rather work the other way around. First we find an object we like and then move things around to accommodate our findings.

**CREATURE COMFORTS** It's easy to fall into the trap of creating interiors without fully addressing your family's true needs. For us, privacy is central. Each of us desires a space where we feel we are in control. An area that is just ours is important—even if it is a simple desk. For our outdoor courtyard, we sought a sanctuary setting and installed a massive wall in order to block the view of new construction. This wall also serves as a backdrop for a tranquil fountain.

**MAKING AN ENTRANCE** We want the entry to our homes to be beautiful and to create a good first impression. Rather than using the entrance as a space to make a large statement, it is a transition point. Most days it seems that our greatest challenge is keeping a neat and tidy entry with two small boys underfoot.

**A BEAUTIFUL BED** We mounted our headboard directly to the wall. For us, this is very practical and it eliminates the need for bed frames, which tend to take up too much space. We use hotel sheeting by Anichini. The Old World craftsmanship, combined with the charm of classic lines and a modern style, is wonderful. Coverlets are great at the foot of the bed, and for decorative touches we like colorful tapestries as bedcovers.

**ENTERTAINING THOUGHTS** Small dinners are much more intimate and preferable to larger gatherings. If more than eight people are invited, we will hire someone to help us during the meal; otherwise we may never get the chance to talk with our guests. September in Mexico is a great time for outdoor parties. We hire a local cook who makes ten types of taco sauces and everyone serves him- or herself. We also enjoy bringing back foods from our travels and inviting friends over for a tasting. The last time we visited Barcelona we brought back two kilos of *pata negra* ham and Manchego cheese for our friends to sample.

# JAMES ANDREW

## STYLE HAS LITTLE TO DO WITH FASHION OR TRENDS. IT IS A WAY OF LIFE AND A REFLECTION OF YOUR GENUINE SELF.

Not many can so elegantly or bravely sport lavender trousers, a Gucci python belt, and silver Dior sneakers and chronicle their daily clothing selections online; but then again few people are James Andrew. To understand and appreciate the man behind the widely popular blog *What Is James Wearing?* you must first let go of any preconceived notions of James or the term "dandy." For the fashion-obsessed interior designer, dandyism goes beyond a basic sartorial fascination—it is a lifestyle. What drives his quest for beauty is an incredible zeal for life and a deep belief that we can create our own reality. Though admittedly obsessed with style and design, he is a caring soul who is just as appealing on the inside. Fashion is merely a creative outlet and only one part of the equation. "My clothes, like my home, are nothing more than a celebration of life."

His apartment may be a "typical" redbrick building in midtown Manhattan, however, the interiors are anything but mainstream. Guests are greeted by glowing red candlestick lamps that once belonged to the Duke and Duchess of Windsor, as well as a holographic silver ceiling in the dining room that casts a rainbow-like pattern over the steel wire table and Frances Elkins loop chairs. Deep-berry lacquered walls, adorned with landscape paintings and a 1970s mirror from Daniel Barney, reside together contentedly. It is not easy to pin down James's aesthetic, but it is clearly grounded in tradition. When pressed to define his sensibility, he opts for a more subjective description, "a sexy version of classic style." His passion for interiors, fashion, architecture, and art all come together beautifully to create a home and life that reflects his multifaceted personality.

**ENTERTAINING THOUGHTS** Entertaining is a great incentive to get my home in order and fill every room with flowers. I personally like small, intimate dinner parties and Sunday luncheons (typically no more than six people). Setting the table and cooking are two of my great passions. I have a few meals that I can whip up in ten minutes when time is not on my side. A great example is wild salmon burgers, steamed asparagus, and salad, served with an ice-cold Sardinian wine. For dessert, simply pair a super-dry white wine with an apple tart tatin. Sometimes simplicity can be your best friend.

**DECORATIVE DETAILS** I have an incredible art collection (mostly the work of friends), and there is something magnificent about my personal connection to the artists. Many of the cherished objects belonged to my mentor, Albert Hadley. Not only do they bring me great pleasure, but they also remind me of all the lessons that I learned from him with regards to design and decoration.

The extravagant beauty and charm of Newport fascinated James as a young boy growing up in Rhode Island. Superb examples of eighteenth- and nineteenth-century architecture, along with the town's famous "summer cottages" ignited a love of houses and a lifelong obsession with design. However, it was a tattered copy of *Vogue* featuring a room designed by Parish-Hadley that captivated his imagination. He was totally enthralled by the beautiful interiors. "I knew at that moment I wanted to be an interior designer." After opting for a more conventional career path of banking and commodities trading, fate finally intervened and set him on a new direction. His boyhood idol, Albert Hadley, invited James to join Parish-Hadley in New York. After working alongside his mentor for two years, he founded his own design firm. Perhaps it is true that how a person masters his fate is more important than what fate ordains.

**FLOWERS AND FRAGRANCES** The aroma of magnolia, gardenia, and tuberose are intoxicating. As for color, I adore shades of pale lavender and deep purples mixed with acid greens, hues that work well in my space. I try to choose candles that seasonally complement the flowers I have in my house. In the spring and summer months, Trianon by Cire Trudon is a must. It's such a perfect balance of roses, herbs, and hyacinth. The candles have been in existence since 1643. Louis XIV, Marie Antoinette, and Napoleon were great enthusiasts. In late autumn and winter, I switch to the woodsy pine scent of Rigaud Cypres.

**A BEAUTIFUL BED** The bedroom is the most personal space in the home and a room where I splurge. A great mattress, well-made linens, and down pillows are a necessity as are generous bedside tables. I prefer tables that can accommodate lamps, books, a glass of water, and flowers. A gorgeous rug is perfect for adding softness and reducing extraneous noise, plus it feels great when you step out of bed. A small writing table, a comfy chair, and photographs of friends, family, and pets round out the mix.

**CREATURE COMFORTS** I am happy in every room of my home. Perhaps it's because I carefully consider each detail, and I love knowing that beautiful, personal objects surround me at all times. For pure comfort and pleasure, I always opt for down-filled sofas and chairs. Another must is tables within easy reach of drinks and lamps near chairs for reading.

**MAKING AN ENTRANCE** I feel an overwhelming sense of gratitude when I come home, and I take great pride in knowing that I designed this space for myself. It is important to create a total sensory experience, not only for my guests but also for myself. My favorite hallway luxuries include a mirror, a place to sit, an umbrella stand, fresh flowers, a burning candle, and soft music. I want for everyone who enters to experience beauty, comfort, and love.

# MARTYN LAWRENCE BULLARD
## DIVERSITY INSPIRES STYLE AND CREATIVITY.

Blessed with incredible charm and a regal edginess, the British-born Martyn Lawrence Bullard leads a fascinating life. His road to decorating fame reads much like a novel. During his childhood, he traveled the world with his family (his father was an opera singer), and by the age of twelve he was roaming flea markets in search of antiques. He later attended the Lee Strasberg Theatre and Film Institute in London's Covent Garden. As a student, Martyn supplemented his income as a runway model before realizing that design was his true calling. "I guess I should have known design was the way to go. I was just a teen when I discovered the virtues of a few yards of fabric and a staple gun. In an hour, I transformed my boyhood bedroom into a tented fantasy fit for a maharaja."

Today, home is a Tuscan-style villa in the Hollywood Hills, which was once the residence of the legendary actor Rudolph Valentino, actress Gloria Swanson, and American writer William Faulkner. By retaining many of the original details, Martyn honors its famous residents of the past. In the dining room, a large, crystal ormolu chandelier, dating to Swanson's tenancy, hangs above an eighteenth-century ebony-and-ivory inlaid table and chairs. Stylized zigzag curtains, made from his own fabric collection, soften the space while adding vibrancy. Playing up the Italian angle, a nod to Valentino, the ceiling is stenciled with a pattern taken from a piece of antique damask found in Venice.

Martyn sees his home as his experiment pad, and is constantly adding new finds and changing the color palette. He views color as a vehicle to infuse personality into his home. Each room is bold and eclectic. Strategic jolts of orange, saffron, sienna red, and olive green, mixed with shades of purple, abound. His selection of

**DECORATIVE DETAILS** My home comes to life with the bounding and loving energy of my beautiful dog, Diva. As for true decorative elements, candles are a must and fill every corner of my home. We all look much better in candlelight. I adore candles so much so that I created my own. Each offers a unique array of exotic, heady, and refreshing scents. In the winter, I long for a roaring fire; it's such a welcoming and atmospheric addition to any room.

**ENTERTAINING THOUGHTS** Sunday evenings are my favorite nights for gathering friends. I adore lashings of cold Pinot Grigio, accompanied by fresh seasonal fruits and full-bodied French cheeses. Leaving decanters of wine and jugs of sparkling water within reach of your guests makes them feel at home. It also makes for a more modern approach to entertaining and keeps even formal, grand dinners a little more lighthearted and fun.

worldly treasures, antiques, and handcrafted possessions are also spectacular and dramatic. Personal and cherished bits and pieces, including photographs, family heirlooms, and objects collected from around the world, create a pleasurable feast for the eye. Milanese furniture from the seventeenth and eighteenth centuries blithely live with a small bronze Rodin. A large collection of photography blends seamlessly with the antiques creating a decorative balance. Works by Herb Ritts, Cecil Beaton, Yul Brynner, Bruce Weber, and Cindy Sherman (some collected and others a gift from Sir Elton John) are scattered throughout each room. Exuberance, a strong command of proportion and scale, and a skillful hand with vibrant hues and bold pattern sum up Martyn's distinguished style. Of all his notable design trademarks, he feels strongly that scale is the most important element of any room, and is of the opinion that this is very hard to achieve. "It's the signature of a seasoned decorator."

**MAKING AN ENTRANCE** Just beyond an old, distressed wooden front door lies an enchanting courtyard—a room unto itself. When I cross the threshold, I feel as if I have been transported to a private oasis. Because it's the first room guests encounter, I decorated the space with furniture that echoes the feeling of my home. It's a magical world at night when completely lit by candles. During the day, the aromas of gardenia and jasmine create a fragrant air that carries throughout my home.

**FLOWERS AND FRAGRANCES** I love cut orchids of every shape and size. Grouped together they create a dramatic effect. Fresh roses in shades of red and white are a staple in my living room. Of course, peonies are a must-have flower when in season, and I cannot resist happy long-stemmed sunflowers in my kitchen. Fragrances in my home usually come from my candles—Vetiver Moresque in the summer and Signature Extraordinaire in the winter. Year round I use amber crystals from L'Artisan Parfumeur to fragrance my drawers and closets.

**A BEAUTIFUL BED** My bed is always layered. In the winter, sheets are folded back over a fine silk and cashmere blanket, with a down comforter at the foot of the bed. In the summer, beautiful lightweight cotton blankets are added for a pop of color. Options range from a cotton or silk woven ikat to a vintage *suzani*. I am slightly obsessed with sheets and have a large collection of linens. Frette sheets, embroidered with either double red or black custom lines, are a favorite. I'm very particular about mattresses. The pure wool mattresses by Vi-Spring are the best.

**CREATURE COMFORTS** I love a deep, comfortable down-filled sofa to curl up on and watch a good movie. Fine Scottish cashmere blankets or throws are vital to my movie-watching ritual as are dimmed lighting, candles, and fragrances. Emotionally, I derive comfort from good food, great friends, and my dog—the ultimate stress relievers.

# THOMAS BURAK AND MICHAEL DEVINE

## WHILE STYLE EVOLVES AND SHIFTS WITH THE TIMES, IT SHOULD NEVER BE CONFUSED WITH THINGS THAT ARE OF THE MOMENT.

Gramercy Park is a rare gem. Elegant brick townhouses, noted for their intricate ironwork, form a square around the private reserve in the middle of Manhattan. A Victorian Gothic building, home to the National Arts Club, is next to the Players Club. Founded by the Shakespearean actor Edwin Booth and brother of John Wilkes Booth, it occupies a wondrous Gothic Revival structure. On the same side of the street, an affable doorman greets guests visiting the elegant apartment of interior designer Thomas Burak and fabric designer Michael Devine. A regular rotation of friends is a common occurrence for the consummate hosts.

Their unsurpassed eye for detail and carefully chosen accessories are apparent the moment you cross the threshold. A long hallway leads you past a beckoning banquette and chairs gathered around a dining table and into a large living room with views of a softly glowing Empire State Building. Table lamps and a roaring fire light and warm up the room. Striking flower arrangements interspersed with books and objects are particularly stunning against silk-lined walls and a palette of dark browns, gold, purple, and gray. It's a room you may never wish to leave once settled in with a book or drink. But despite the comfortable ambiance, like many New Yorkers, Thomas and Michael long to escape the city on the weekend.

**DECORATIVE DETAILS** We both adore books. Each title reveals something very personal about our interests. Stacked atop a chair or table, they can further enrich a room. Meaningful objects that we've purchased on our travels or the fun little gifts that we've given each other over the years are among our favorite details. Decorative elements such as the passementerie on a pillow or a piece of Michael's fabric also add a special touch to our homes. "Less is more" are not words that ever pass our lips.

When hunting for a country retreat, the couple found a charming 1840s building in the village of Kinderhook, New York. Though not a typical weekend home, it is situated on the historic town green and had space for Michael to expand his burgeoning fabric company as well as a lovely backyard garden. With its quirky cottage charm, indoor-outdoor living spaces, and studio, the house appealed to them both immediately. While renovation was required, they maintained much of the enchanting eccentricities—particularly the small rooms. However, some of the ceilings were raised to add variation to the layout. A palette of fresh, crisp greens, Wedgwood blues, navy, and white, along with Michael's fabrics, take center stage.

In tight quarters measuring 25 feet wide by 120 feet deep, and wishing to indulge their passion for gardening, Michael looked to the formal grounds at Paris's Rodin Museum for inspiration and rolled up his sleeves. A prefabricated shed, customized with French doors and a thatched-style roof, stands at the far end of the yard, ready for outdoor drinks and dining. Michael draped the walls and table with his linen fabrics and hung a flea-market candlelight chandelier. On summer nights, it is the perfect spot for hosting guests, and, in the early morning hours, it is a relaxing place to sit and have a cup of coffee.

**MAKING AN ENTRANCE** An entryway is the first opportunity to make guests feel welcome. Creating a gracious environment helps set the tone. Proper lighting, fresh seasonal flowers, and wonderful smells are elements that say, "Welcome." Although our two homes are quite different in style, our needs and those of our guests are the same. A closet for coats, a table for keys, and a place for a visitor to rest his or her tote bag is a must. But most important, you need a defined space to greet your guests. In the city, we have a long hallway with a bar niche—it is the perfect spot to pause and offer friends a drink.

**A BEAUTIFUL BED** Freshly laundered, pressed sheets are a must, as are down pillows and a down duvet. Most of the year we use Frette percale sheets with contrasting color embroidery and hem-stitched cuffs on the pillowcases. During cooler months in the country, we opt for the heavy, antique French linen sheets purchased during a trip to Normandy. In Manhattan, a custom-block quilted down cover, folded at the foot of the bed on top of the duvet, is wonderfully warm in the winter. Other bedroom essentials include convenient night tables, good lighting, and fresh flowers.

## FLOWERS AND FRAGRANCES

The fragrances in our homes typically come from fresh flowers, especially in Kinderhook, where we have an abundant flowering garden. In our apartment, there is always a rotation of fragrances throughout the growing season, and for a few precious weeks each June heirloom roses scent the air. Other treasured varieties include cosmos, bachelor buttons, parrot tulips, hydrangeas, and white nicotiana. For candles, Diptyque is always beautifully scented; Lilac in spring, Foin Coupé in summer, and Feu de Bois for autumn and winter are favorites.

## ENTERTAINING THOUGHTS We

love to entertain. Summers in Kinderhook make life wonderfully easy, as all we have to do is go to the garden and find everything that we need from lettuces to herbs and fruits to flowers. In the city, we always host dinner parties in our apartment. The norm for New Yorkers is cocktails at home followed by dinner out, so a meal at home is a great treat for our guests. Michael takes over the kitchen while I fuss with the table and flowers. Sometimes we serve casual lap dinners on pretty trays by the fire in the living room.

## JESSE CARRIER AND MARA MILLER
### STYLISH LIVING IS EATING DINNER WITH YOUR KIDS AT THE DINING TABLE AND ALLOWING THEM TO MAKE FORTS WITH YOUR CASHMERE THROWS AND DOWN-FILLED SOFA CUSHIONS.

Charming simplicity, classic picture-rail molding, original hardware, plank wood flooring, and high ceilings are precisely what drew husband and wife Jesse Carrier and Mara Miller to their prewar Manhattan apartment. The sunlit 900-square-foot home with beautiful views of the East River is an added bonus. For the busy parents and in-demand interior designers, they understand the challenges of designing for an active family. The couple also know full well that small children, pets, and hectic schedules can undermine the desire to live stylishly, yet they manage the task very well.

Known for their edited, clean, and classic style, the husband-and-wife team has found many fans and clients in the fashion world, including Anna Wintour and fashion designer Jason Wu. Their ability to create timeless, rather than trendy interiors, is part of their appeal. Influenced by the diversity and harmonizing mix of the old and new that they experience living in the city, they compose calming yet interesting interiors. And both strongly believe that editing is always crucial to good design, especially when space is at a premium. This philosophy is evident in their own environment, as are good doses of organization and design flexibility. Dual-purpose furniture, such as a chest of drawers on either side of their sofa that double as toy storage and the often-underutilized stool, abound. The stool is a particular favorite due to its ability to gracefully convert into extra seating, a cocktail table, or a place to rest your feet. "Plus, it is very mobile and compact," Mara notes.

The sophisticated feeling of their home is achieved primarily through well-appointed accessories and artwork rather than an overuse of upholstered furnishings. A thrift-shop

**FLOWERS AND FRAGRANCES** Potted paper whites are a seasonal favorite. Red-currant-scented candles by Votivo are a staple in our home and sandalwood incense is burned on occasion. As for fragrances and flowers, a seasonal change is good. We love the smell and sight of peonies in the spring and summer, but like woodsy aromas in fall and winter. Peonies are wonderful for their abundant bouquet, and hydrangea and tulips for their lovely appearance. We avoid arrangements and generally opt for single species amassed in big bunches.

Venetian chandelier and vintage brass lamp bounce soft light off the lacquered walls of their welcoming hallway and spotlight family photos nestled in the bookcases. The light-reflecting paint, along with carefully placed mirrors, makes the space feel much larger and adds instant sparkle. "It is easier to express your interests by updating your interiors through accessories," notes Jesse.

But perhaps where they excel is their uncanny ability to communicate not only with clients but also each other. Both are of the mind that a house can be impeccably designed and decorated to the nines, but will fall short and feel stagnant without the energy that comes from living in every room. They do acknowledge that rugs get threadbare from traffic, sofas get worn out from movie nights, and tablecloths need replacing because of too many wine stains, but they agree that these are the very elements that make a house a home.

**MAKING AN ENTRANCE** We painted our entry walls with a high-gloss lacquer finish in a dark, warm taupe color. While the darker tone helps create the impression of a sizeable space, it also provides a stark contrast from the considerably larger and light-filled adjacent living room. The lacquer finish gives sparkle to a windowless room. Our goal was to create a subtle and integral space. We hope that guests feel that they are welcome and consider this space not simply a place to hang their coats.

**DECORATIVE DETAILS** An unexpected mix and display of artwork wakes up our walls. Pots of flowers and stacks of books are always inviting. We like juxtaposition and pieces that serve multiple purposes. Our upholstered settee in the window paired with a vintage marble-topped Tulip table (complete with rusted base) is a great example. This area is used throughout the day for breakfast, puzzles, homework, and crafts, and the settee is the perfect perch to sit and enjoy the view or a cup of coffee.

**A BEAUTIFUL BED** White or cream cotton percale sheeting is our favorite, and we especially adore Sferra. Macy's Hotel Collection is also a good basic sheeting. We add two sets of pillows (one soft and one firm) and a textured coverlet with a down duvet comforter folded at the foot of the bed, plus two to four decorative pillows. We never embellish the bed with more than four pillows; getting into bed shouldn't be a chore.

**ENTERTAINING THOUGHTS** A summer picnic or a barbecue is our favorite way to entertain family and friends. If pressed for time, we will just order in and keep it simple. Dimmed lights, music for atmosphere, and handblown glasses (even for the simplest of drinks) are a must. Often we rotate meals and feed the children first while adults have cocktails; then we let the children play while the grown-ups enjoy dinner. Small space living does require strategy; however, compromise is not necessary.

## TAMMY CONNOR

### I GRAVITATE TOWARD HOMES AND PEOPLE
### THAT ARE INVITING, WARM, AND AUTHENTIC.

Growing up in the Hollywood area of Birmingham, Alabama, Tammy Connor often visited the 1926 Tudor she now calls home. The residential subdivision, built in the 1920s as a summering spot, lured many Birmingham residents over the ridge of Red Mountain. The new homes were predominately English Tudor and Spanish Colonial Revival styles that were fashionably linked with the glamour of Hollywood, Florida. "This house was always my favorite in the neighborhood. I often played here as a little girl," she recalls. After living in Charleston, South Carolina, for several years and establishing her design firm, family connections and sentiment drew Tammy back home.

Before setting up house, she and her husband, Geoff, embarked on a nine-month-long restoration. Longing to bring the structure back to its original grandeur while adding modern conveniences, Tammy took inspiration from houses in the surrounding historic neighborhood. Although the majority of updates were aesthetic in nature, careful attention was given to functionality and spatial balance. Floors were replaced with hardwood, custom cabinetry was installed, and painted interior stone was brought back to its natural state. Staying true to her reputation for creating classic homes infused with Southern elegance and charm, Tammy added flickering gas lanterns, shapely boxwoods, and bluestone to the exterior. A new brick-lined drive was laid, the entrance was replaced with pavers, and the graceful allée of holly trees, leading from the house to the pool, was revitalized. The garden and pool are places where Tammy entertains often, as the Birmingham climate invites outdoor living most of the year. Even on the warmest of days her children play outside, while screen doors are open to capture the sound of laughter and smell of confederate jasmine that trails around windows.

**MAKING AN ENTRANCE** With an entryway that is only five feet by five feet, it is all about intimacy. To make the most of the sunny spot, I added a window seat, a small chandelier, and a petite antique chair. Currently, I would love to have a highly functional mudroom for my kids. It would be great to have a place that is organized, complete with a family craft table, gift-wrapping station, and a place to hide toys.

   Equally important to Tammy was to design a family home that was inviting and visually interesting. The original entryway afforded visitors with little more than a narrow passageway from the front door to the living room. To make this space welcoming, she added a cheerful window seat and a charming diminutive chandelier. Unceremonious antiques, carefully selected art, comfortable furnishings, crisp linens, soft slipcovers, delicate embroidery, and a neutral color scheme help create a feeling of calmness and visually link each room. The peaceful backdrop is the perfect stage for her many collections including antique vellum books, one-of-a-kind pillows made from old textiles and vintage Fortuny fabric, and unusual creamware pieces. A delicate Fortuny chandelier, purchased in Venice, hangs above a rustic dining room table, which is surrounded by ladder-backed chairs dressed up in skirts tied with grosgrain ribbon. "Antiques provide a sense of history and their craftsmanship is difficult to replicate," says Tammy. Light custom paint colors add depth and richness to rough stucco walls, and sea-grass rugs further soften hardwood floors. A firm believer that a timeless color palette is inspired by nature, the designer relies on neutrals, greens, and blues to create a foundation for her rooms. It is both Tammy's ingenuity and a mixture of textures that keep her Tudor from feeling "heavy" or too dark.

Yet nothing in the house is so precious that it can't be touched or enjoyed. "I don't let my aesthetic decisions dictate the way we live. I fully realize that things may get ruined from time to time." Perfectly appointed for all family members, few things in the Connor home are off-limits to their two young children and springer spaniel. In fact, Tammy counts her daughter's pale-pink room among her favorite places to spend time with her children. It is also the room that holds some of her most treasured objects—clay crosses. All of the bisque-colored crosses were handmade by friends at her first baby shower. Each person was given a hunk of clay and a few tools. "When I look at the wall, I can see their personality in each one. I always feel like my friends are around me when I am at home."

**FLOWERS AND FRAGRANCES** I always have fresh flowers or a candle nearby. I also love to clip flowering branches or anything that is blooming in the garden. Peonies, gardenias, and 'Casablanca' lilies are among my favorites. During the winter months and around Christmastime, I enjoy the lingering scents of mandarin, clove, pine, and eucalyptus. The combination of spice and evergreen instantly marks the start of the holidays. In the warmer months, I leave the windows open so that the natural aromas of spring and summer can seep in.

**A BEAUTIFUL BED** I like to be nestled between layers of sheets and a down comforter, with the dog at my feet (even in the summer). Ironed cotton percale bed linens are the ultimate luxury. I prefer to unwind from the day by reading, doing paperwork, and writing in my bed. One of the things that I love most about our bedroom is the moonlight on the pool below— the reflections dance on the walls at night, making it so incredibly peaceful.

**CREATURE COMFORTS** Hot tea, long walks, freshly laundered linens, and a stack of inspirational books on the bedside table are simple indulgences that always make me feel at home. As for my emotional well-being, fresh flowers, family photos, the first night home after traveling, and a color-coordinated closet give me the false sense that the chaos of an active lifestyle is all under control.

**ENTERTAINING THOUGHTS** I love a candlelit outdoor gathering on a warm summer evening. Lanterns hanging from the trees and scents of lavender, jasmine, and rosemary add just the right amount of romance. Often we entertain family and friends by the pool. The adults relax and grill on the terrace, and the children swim. I always like to be prepared, but I'm never too serious. Hospitality and a sense of humor is all you really need.

# FLORENCE DE DAMPIERRE
## I STRIVE TO LIVE LIFE IN A JOYOUS, COLORFUL, AND STYLISH MANNER.

In a sea of white historical New England homes in Litchfield, Connecticut, Florence de Dampierre's imposing nineteenth-century dwelling stands out from the rest. Not for its sheer size, but rather its bright lime-green door and the stylish French hostess who enthusiastically welcomes guests. A leopard-patterned carpet spanning the entryway and winding up the large staircase further confirms that this is no ordinary house. And while the decor is decidedly French in nature, it is not fashioned in a stereotypical way. You won't find a plethora of overly gilded Louis XIV furniture (though gold touches do exist), nor is there an abundance of Provençal fruitwood chairs. Rather, the decor is an eclectic mix of classic and contemporary furnishings from around the world. Elegant and witty, each room notes Florence's own version of joie de vivre. "The French really do have a legendary sense of style that is synonymous with a joyous, sophisticated way of life. This is just the way I like to live," she affirms.

Florence counts nearly every shade of green, orange, and purple among her favorite colors, and each has a strong presence in her home. In the library, the heart of the house, green and orange take center stage. The walls are washed in a pale shade of green, as is the fireplace and woodwork. A line of "punchy Hermès" orange, painted just below the green crown molding, adds a touch of flamboyance to this upbeat space. Beyond the library, a terrace leading from the living room gives full views of the gardens, pool, and wooded lot beyond the expansive yard. "I spend many happy hours in my study overlooking our pool and the vine-covered trellis leading to the topiary garden. It's my personal heaven."

**FLOWERS AND FRAGRANCES** I love all flowers, but my favorites are hyacinth, paper whites, delphinium, peonies, and mimosa. Plants are also an essential component in bringing a room to life, not to mention the fresh scent is an added bonus. For a witty and architectural touch, I designed a line of topiaries made of natural moss, based on a seventeenth-century design; they are both chic and whimsical.

In addition to designing, writing, and launching a recent furniture line, the antiques expert is also an accomplished cook and hostess. Once the weather turns warm, you will find Florence in the garden clipping chives or serving lunch at the pool house. Freshly grown vegetables are always on the menu, from vibrant red radishes to juicy plum tomatoes (a key ingredient in her much-loved tomato tart). Entertaining is one of her great pleasures. "In all matters, decorating, entertaining, or otherwise, I am a great believer in mixing high and low elements." The pool house table, surrounded by simple chairs (stenciled by Florence), and set with French Sèvres plates, is a prime example of her style and ability. When time allows, you will find the perpetually busy designer relaxing by the pool, singing along with Carla Bruni and dreaming up her next project.

Other obsessions include dark chocolates with sea salt and caramel and fashion. "I am crazy about clothes! But shoes and accessories are my real weakness." Once named to Eleanor Lambert's best-dressed list, Florence fills the closet of her toile de jouy bedroom with everything from high-heeled Manolo Blahnik boots, Repetto flats, and Topshop sweaters to Zara dresses, Prada jackets, and fur-lined gloves. "Fashion is like design; you own a couple of great pieces and then you fill in the gaps with simple jeans and some fun, flirty dresses." Her joyous outlook is completely compatible with her chic style and buoyant approach to life.

**MAKING AN ENTRANCE** To make an entrance, you need to banish all fears, starting with the front door. I love an element of surprise. For entryways, I favor overscaled objects such as an obelisk or sculpture and walls painted in a vibrant color and covered with intimate ensembles of charming artwork. I also believe that the most inviting interiors are filled with personal mementos. The soft aqua-colored walls of my hallway are a peaceful and inviting backdrop for the leopard-patterned carpet, which is playful, stain resistant, and very forgiving.

**ENTERTAINING THOUGHTS** Entertaining is a year-round joy. In the summer, I adore leisurely lunches by the pool, and in the winter, I serve dinner by a roaring fire. Each season offers its own unique pleasures. Dinner parties are always great fun and a bit like a play—therefore a great backdrop is essential. However, decor is only one part of the equation; an interesting cast of characters is a must in order to create the perfect mix. Planning ahead so that your event looks effortless is so important, as is tried-and-true recipes, beautifully plated food, and lots of alcohol.

**DECORATIVE DETAILS** It's the little details that imbue my home with personality. The pool house living room perfectly illustrates the unexpected mix of high and low objects and furnishings that I prefer. This kind of decorative ensemble creates a textured look that is visually interesting. Comfortable sofas are enhanced with custom-made pillows finished with trim. A backdrop of shelving and cabinetry displays botanicals and contemporary and classical works of art along with whimsical objects intermingled with important pieces including antique Wedgwood and terra-cotta and marble busts.

**A BEAUTIFUL BED** A comfortable bed is the reward at the end of a long day. White sheets, enhanced with a soft duvet, comforter, or throw (in cashmere or fur) are essential. Lately, I am obsessed with white linen sheets trimmed with a small border. The trim provides just the right hint of color.

## BARRY DIXON

### FEW THINGS ARE BETTER THAN LIVING AN AUTHENTIC LIFE AND SHARING THAT WORLD WITH OTHERS.

It takes a special person to set up home in a notable house and take on the role of caretaker. Interior designer Barry Dixon has been the owner of historic Elway Hall for more than thirteen years. He is no stranger to living in fascinating homes or far-flung places. Though Barry was born in Memphis, Tennessee, his father's job took the Dixon family around the world. With each move, he learned to assimilate and blend seemingly incongruent cultures and objects into a bespoke reality.

Barry first happened upon his picturesque Edwardian-style estate in Warrenton, Virginia, aboard an airport shuttle. After flipping through a dog-eared real estate brochure featuring the 20,000-square-foot manor, he recognized an impending move was on the horizon. Within five days, he and his late partner, Michael Schmidt, bought the property. Built in 1907 by West Virginia senator Johnson Newlon Camden, the house was constructed for his only daughter, Mrs. Baldwin Day Spilman, as a wedding gift.

Almost a century later the leaded-glass Tiffany windows and seventeen fireplaces are still intact. Before Barry and Michael first viewed the house, it had undergone a pristine restoration. Blackened woodwork had been stripped to its natural state and immense stretches of wall were sanded. It was a blank slate just waiting to come to life. While some "freshening up" was required, not a single mantel or original feature was changed. "With a grand dame you don't try to reinvent her, but rather you just keep her in shape."

Barry's design philosophy, rooted in tradition, was the perfect match for the rambling residence. Always mixing high and low with old and new, he is careful to

**DECORATIVE DETAILS** Personal collections reveal the soul of the homeowner. Treasures that I cannot live without include books, working fireplaces, color, cocktail stations, candles, natural arrangements of flowers, polished silver, gleaming glassware, dogs, worn leather, ottomans, seasonal smells, views, a piano, and laughter.

listen to a room's visual suggestions before moving forward with a design. He is not shy about spending money on objects that are rare and enjoy great character, but feels that he must "earn the right" by also introducing less expensive items. "The most important things in a room are the essence of what we hold valuable. A room should start a conversation before people ever exchange words."

The home's great hall, music room, sitting room, and library spill from the imposing foyer and sweeping carved oak staircase. Each space leads to another more fascinating and interesting spot. It is a layout geared for grand parties and socializing. Upstairs, the 118-foot-long oak-planked hallway stretches the entire transverse axis of the house. Nine guest bedrooms (all used for frequent houseguests) line the long corridor. Each bedroom has its own fireplace, and during the holidays, a Christmas tree adorns every one.

Though large and impressive, it is a warm and welcoming home. Set on 300 acres, with a barn and livestock, Elway has the integrity of a great country house. The tradition of the English hunt played a role in designing the house and certainly weighed on the mind of the original owner, who was a founding member of the Warrenton Hunt. For a better part of a century, social gatherings were an important part of Elway's history; the doors were always open to friend and family for hunt breakfasts and holidays. Barry still keeps both traditions alive. Breakfast is his favorite time to entertain. Having a full henhouse, he hasn't served store-bought eggs in ten years.

**MAKING AN ENTRANCE** You only get one chance to make a first impression, so you want to get it right. An entrance should feel gracious, inviting, elegant, and personal. It should foster a sense of warmth and hospitality; it's the liaison between the sacred inside and the world outside. The best entryways don't give away the whole secret of the home but rather leave a little mystery and romance.

**CREATURE COMFORTS** Single malt scotch, a roaring fire, a steeping tub of hot water, Rancé leather-scented soap, and my wire-haired fox terrier, Ellie, stretched out in a dead sleep provide great comfort. Sitting outside at dusk in Adirondack chairs lined up on my lawn, with a cocktail resting on their broad, flat, paddle arm, is heaven; or the same scenario at dawn—just substitute cocktails for coffee.

### FLOWERS AND FRAGRANCES

I like flowers that are indigenous to my corner of the world. I have a half-acre cutting garden that yields flowers and boughs nine months out of the year. During the winter months, I cut lots of evergreen, magnolia, juniper, and cedar. The peony is my favorite flower for both sight and scent, but lilac and mock orange tie for a close second. I never tire of the color, texture, and effect of viburnum branches.

### ENTERTAINING THOUGHTS

I love to have weekend guests. I fête them with a huge country breakfast, light suppers, and long walks around the farm. December is my favorite month for entertaining. I traditionally host a holiday party the first Saturday of the month. Roaring fires blaze in all seventeen fireplaces and the piano rings out holiday carols in the music room. My greatest entertaining tip is bars, bars, bars—everyone loves a cocktail! Splurge on the best to keep all in good spirits.

### A BEAUTIFUL BED

For ultimate comfort, I tuck a down and feather duvet filler between the mattress and the fitted sheet, all of which is topped off with a flat sheet and down comforter. I prefer the softness of sateen sheets for most of the year. When it is especially warm outside, I switch to crisp flaxen linen that has been pressed with light starch and trade my duvet for a cotton quilt at the foot of the bed.

## TOBI FAIRLEY
### STYLISH LIVING ISN'T ABOUT PUTTING ON A PERFORMANCE FOR GUESTS, BUT RATHER ENJOYING THE THINGS YOU LOVE WHEN YOU ARE ALONE.

Tobi Fairley believes in handwritten thank-you notes on heavy cardstock, properly placed silver, home-cooked meals, and the virtues of a friendly smile. The gracious Arkansas designer lives her life in a manner that is reflected in her traditional two-story home. Set against a tree-lined street and the rolling hills of Little Rock, the house exhibits many qualities of a quintessential American home. However, once you open the front door, an explosion of dramatic color assures you that it is anything but typical. Sweeping black-and-white damask wallpaper draws you into a welcoming retreat. Kelly green, shades of cream, and hints of gold infuse the sunny living room just off the entryway. A starburst mirror above a raw silk sofa further reflects the bold paper and gleaming sunlight, giving the room a warm glow.

The abundant space and traffic patterns are precisely what drew Tobi and her husband, Carter, to their home. "We love to entertain and I adore how all of the rooms open up to each other. It's a wonderful place for parties." The house is treated like a whole rather than a series of individual areas; the result is a seamless transition between rooms. Shades of green and black are carried into the inviting family room that is infused with a zesty orange. It was not a shade Tobi had planned on using until she fell in love with a pair of orange lamps. A lacquered bench followed and soon an orange upholstered wing chair, trimmed in white welting, made its debut.

An open, circular floor plan leads guests from the living to the family quarters and adjacent dining room—areas that are in frequent use. A pair of double French doors in the family room opens directly onto a large back patio, doubling the space for

**FLOWERS AND FRAGRANCES** Nest's Bamboo candles are amazing. I also love the classic, fresh scent of Diptyque's Fig candle, especially in the green mouth-blown glass jar. The pink peony is unrivaled in its ability to deliver drama. Its soft romantic form, cheerful color, and lovely scent brighten any room. For color alone, blue hydrangeas, orange tulips, and pink rhododendrons are wonderful.

entertaining. Wishing to use drapery for both light control and decoration, hinged French drapery rods were installed to allow for easy opening without inhibiting traffic flow or obstructing the view. The interiors are composed of many traditional furnishings with a modern twist. Dining chairs have been updated with floral and crewel upholstery, while the seats are covered in chartreuse vinyl, making them chic and kid friendly. A wall of framed botanical prints mirrors the natural beauty outside, and a lantern chandelier provides a playful touch.

When not "nesting" (a much-loved preoccupation), you will find Tobi in her bright, white kitchen on the phone with her mother or cooking with her young daughter, Ellison. Family favorites include chicken and dumplings, sweet tea, and prize-worthy cakes and pies baked from her mother and grandmother's recipes. "There is nothing I like more than being at home surrounded by the people and the things that I love."

**MAKING AN ENTRANCE** The entryway is like an invitation to a party; it sets the tone for all that is to come. Comfort is very important to me and I want my family and guests to feel as if they can put their feet up without guilt. Perhaps it's the nurturer in me, but I also think great smells coming from the kitchen are so welcoming.

**DECORATIVE DETAILS** Comfortable furnishings, colorful fabrics, and accessories are a must. Dramatic wallpaper, bold patterns, drapery on every window, custom rugs, and original artwork are equally important. I have a large collection that is truly personal; with many of the pieces collected on my travels. Favorite artists include Kansas City native Jane Booth, New Orleans–based Steve Martin, and Arkansas artists Sheila Cotton, Arden Boyce, Marc Hatfield, and Virginia McKimmey.

**A BEAUTIFUL BED** I adore Legna sheets by SDH made from Italian wood fiber. They are softer than silk but wear like cotton. And best yet, they don't have to be ironed all the time. I need lots of down pillows and layers. I can't sleep without the weight of covers, even in the summer months. White sheets are a staple, but I change my blankets with the season.

**CREATURE COMFORTS** Flowers, hot tea, sparkling water, writing and sketching in pretty journals, magazines, crisply ironed cotton pajamas, raw almonds, dark chocolate, artwork purchased during my travels, yoga, meditating, and prayer all contribute to my sense of emotional and physical well-being. A collection of favorite wines in storage and a stack of books on my bedside table make me very happy.

**ENTERTAINING THOUGHTS** I prefer seated and plated dinners to buffet style. I like to set a formal table using my grandmother's china, monogrammed linens, menu cards, and place cards. Place cards written in gorgeous penmanship is like art for the table. The season always dictates the tablescape, flowers, linens, and, of course, the menu. I have a passion for wine and love pairing it with great food. My newfound love is Red Stitch wine, which was introduced to me by my friend Tricia Roberts. She and her husband, both sommeliers, started the company with two other couples in Napa, California. Although they have a small bottling, each year I find a way to get my hands on at least a few of their Cabernet.

# BRIAN PATRICK FLYNN
## ALWAYS SURROUND YOURSELF WITH THINGS THAT INSPIRE AND REFLECT YOUR POINT OF VIEW.

If you think that a lack of space limits creativity, look no further than Brian Patrick Flynn's 750-square-foot midcentury modern Hollywood Hills apartment. The all-American, playful designer can pack a punch when it comes to fun and color. Unexpected vintage toys and youthful Pop art dial back the seriousness of beautifully tailored fabrics and plush rugs. A piece of "found art," an acrylic Circle K sign, hangs above a tulip table and Saarinen chairs. While growing up in Fort Lauderdale, Brian spent many happy days at the local Circle K stocking up on snacks before heading to the beach. "I have so many great memories of those years, and this quirky sign brings a bit of soul to my dining room."

The interior designer recently became bicoastal when he moved his interior design firm from Atlanta to Los Angeles, in part due to his role as design producer of HGTV's *Design Star* (he still keeps a place in Georgia). His new home is packed with preppy plaids, tartans, strong graphics, Hamptons-esque nautical stripes, and whitewashed wood floors. A plethora of some-love-it-and-others-are-scared-of-it vintage art, including tennis rackets, horns, and plastic peacocks blanket the walls. If you can imagine Ralph Lauren moving in with the Royal Tenenbaums, then you come close to understanding Brian's personality and style.

**DECORATIVE DETAILS** Contrasting accent colors can really bring a room to life. In my apartment, fire-engine red plays off shades of blue. Overall, blue is very soothing, but the vibrancy of the red adds a ton of energy; it makes the traditional calm color a bit more exciting. Unique vintage art adds personality as well. None of the pieces are too serious, but they contribute to a certain whimsy. One detail I'll never forgo is custom upholstery; like a couture dress, such a finish makes everything look better.

He considers "safe" to be one of the most horrid of four-letter words in decorating, and admires those who are not afraid to break the rules—especially if the results are beautiful and thought provoking. Brian is turned on by curiosity, kindness, and a genuine interest in others. Perhaps his natural disposition is the reason that he gravitates towards "happy colors" in his home. His first choice is always blue, followed by orange and red. Once you enter Brian's domain, you feel like staying, kicking off your shoes, getting comfy, talking, and laughing a lot. Brian's ability to communicate warmth through his designs makes you want to linger, but mostly it's his playful, good-natured personality.

**MAKING AN ENTRANCE** Once guests walk through the door, they are standing directly in my living room. A floor-to-ceiling picture window and sofa offer a warm and welcoming sunny spot for friends to relax. Whenever a home lacks a true entrance, I like to play up architectural assets so that the eye sees something spectacular. My window frames a beautiful lush garden, and seeing palm trees the moment the door opens is pretty amazing.

**FLOWERS AND FRAGRANCES** I often burn exotic, woodsy scented candles. However, in the summer, I like freshly scented ones that remind me of rainwater, an ocean breeze, or fresh linen. As for flowers, aesthetically, the peony is my favorite (especially in shades of coral), but tulips are my daily choice. Sometimes I like to come home to blooming hyacinths as they make everything seem so fresh and laundered.

**A BEAUTIFUL BED** The only time that my bed is perfectly made is when I invite guests over. I have no idea why I stress over the bed at these times—it's not as if they are eating chicken at the foot of my bed. When the bed is set to perfection, I use four pillows (two on each side of the bed and stacked two deep). Then I layer two large thirty-by-thirty-inch overstuffed down throw pillows and a smaller twenty-two-by-twenty-two-inch throw pillow in the middle. The duvet is usually turned down. I love overscaled, hefty table lamps on each side of the bed.

**CREATURE COMFORTS** I believe that having greenery and fresh flowers throughout my apartment is great for keeping the air clean. Sticking to one bold color for each room keeps me happy. If I visit a home that is all cream or "tone on tone" and neutral, I start to get antsy.

**ENTERTAINING THOUGHTS** My favorite way to entertain family and friends is buffet style. Just put everything out in bowls or on trays and let people come and go as they please. I definitely believe that everything looks better on a tray. Spring is a wonderful time to gather friends; everyone is getting out of their hibernating mode and ready to socialize. I just open the windows, serve cocktails, and order takeout. Often the best times are the ones that are impromptu and not overly planned.

## MAUREEN FOOTER
### LIFE IS INTRINSICALLY RICH. IT'S ABOUT APPRECIATING WHAT YOU HAVE AND NOT ALWAYS LOOKING TO ACQUIRE MORE.

Walking into Maureen Footer's Upper East Side studio apartment reminds me of lifting the lid on my childhood jewelry box and watching the perfectly poised ballerina twirl among the pink compartments. Much like my beloved jewelry box, Maureen's space is small, but exceedingly charming and filled with beautiful treasures. It comes as no surprise that the passionate hostess and former investment banker once wanted to be a dance critic. "I've always loved ballet. When I was at Wellesley, there was a professor with the most amazing use of language who wrote for *Dance Review.* His writing was so vivid you didn't even have to go to the ballet to visualize every detail. It made a huge impression on me and my life."

Always a lover of beauty, language, and the arts, Maureen found herself in Paris at the age of thirty, with her nose pressed against every antique dealer's window in the Carré Rive Gauche. On the eve of her departure from Paris, she sat on the bed in her hotel room and realized her calling was to exercise her fascination with interiors and creating rooms that would enrich the lives of others. "I have always believed that how we define our home is the most personal expression of who we are," she reflects, thinking of that career-changing day. Maureen's own home, filled with antiques and rich splashes of color, is a testament to that belief and her personal convictions. Once the Matisse-like hues of the jewel box apartment envelop you, it's difficult to imagine any other profession more suited to the accomplished decorator and historian. Signs of a distinct personality are everywhere, from Venetian pink walls to sterling-silver kitchen accessories and the jingling of her charm bracelet as she serves trays of smoked salmon to guests.

**DECORATIVE DETAILS** Memories, music, inspiration, conversation, and ideas add soul to my home. What brings it all to life is color, floor-to-ceiling books, French furniture, and objects from my travels. Whether it's a Tang dynasty figure, an Indian oil lamp purchased in the brass market in Jaipur, or an enamel elephant from Udaipur, each object is special and represents memories of a joyous life. I would be so unhappy if a sense of past and the continuum of time were missing from my home. The one detail that I will never forgo is something old and beautiful with personal significance.

**ENTERTAINING THOUGHTS** When you bring together the perfect mix of people, magic will happen. Years ago a friend told me that a dinner party is a gift that you give to others. I love to create an atmosphere that is conducive to conversation. I try to be strategic about finding a menu that allows me maximum time with my guests, so I am always looking for interesting recipes that don't require lots of last-minute sautéing and fussing. Navarins, curries, and fish en papillote fit the bill perfectly.

It was also in Paris, while pursuing graduate studies in eighteenth-century decorative arts, that she realized the powerful influence of Enlightenment principles and the arts—a blending of the classics, sensuality, and beauty with quintessentially progressive thoughts. The talented San Francisco native and connoisseur of eighteenth-century French antiques is a self-proclaimed preservationist and makes no apologies for being "a tree-hugging environmentalist," who is obsessive about recycling. "Antiques are my favorite recycled items and I adore candlelight. It's much prettier than fluorescent bulbs," she laughs. Her point is well taken, and her home is living proof that antiques are not only beautiful but also relevant, tangible reminders that the human race's aspirations and innovations have been going strong for thousands of years and continue to endure.

**MAKING AN ENTRANCE** I love being at home and I am delighted when I return at the end of a day. Even in my small apartment, I have tried to create a defined and welcoming entry space by using hand-painted custom wallpaper and bright Chinese red woodwork that is reflected in a magical gilt-wood mirror. I find mirrors to be extraordinary. They reflect light, multiply space, and glitter. Of course, they are fabulous for the last-minute check as you run out the door.

**FLOWERS AND FRAGRANCES** I adore candles that linger, and I tend to stay consistent when it comes to scents. That said, I think it's fun to have a little change when someone brings me a new candle. But I always go back to my stalwart—Diptyque Figuier. It's a wonderfully light and breezy year-round scent. However, in the depth of winter, I usually burn Rigaud Cypres. It's a refreshing and natural fragrance that was the signature candle of the Kennedy White House. Tulips are by far my favorite flower. I adore everything about them—the way the stems arch, the color of the leaves, their visual strength, and their very subtle outdoorsy scent.

**A BEAUTIFUL BED** I use white percale sheets all year long. I find percale to be so serene, cool, and inviting. Of course, being a lover of color, I usually have some embroidered details in a soft shade. I need down pillows for sleeping and piles of pillows for reading and taking notes in my journal each night. In the winter, I always use a duvet cover to match my linens, then I switch it out for a summer blanket in the warmer months. But no matter the season, I have the peculiar American habit of using a top sheet under the duvet or blanket. Apparently, this custom confounds the Austrians.

**CREATURE COMFORTS** Calm and order certainly contribute toward my sense of well-being. Life is frenetic so at home I love to create the illusion that all is calm. The evenings after my housekeeper has come are paradise. Coffee on a silver tray in the morning is my simple yet wonderful ritual. I take it to my desk on weekdays as I read the *New York Times*, and on the weekend, I bring it back to bed. I also use as little paper as possible, so over time I have acquired a collection of monogrammed napkins that I use every day.

# BRAD FORD

## FEW THINGS ARE MORE IMPORTANT THAN CONFIDENCE. IT IS WHAT ALLOWS YOU TO FULLY EXPRESS YOURSELF AND YOUR BELIEFS.

Sixteen floors above the hurried streets of Chelsea, on the West Side of Manhattan, Brad Ford has skillfully carved out an oasis of calm amid the chaos of the city below. Neutral tones, grounded by a cement floor painted chocolate brown, dominate the sunny living area of his apartment. A bronze bird sits atop a carved stool and a *Planet of the Apes* print by the London-based artist Von hangs above a wooden desk and vintage Eames desk chair. There is a lighthearted, midcentury quality to many of the pieces that fill the apartment; shelves brim with organic objects, playful art lines the walls, and clean shapes give the space balance. His aesthetic is easy and effortless with a modern slant. To avoid a stark ambiance, Brad has carefully selected subtle textures and natural materials that add softness.

Growing up in a small Arkansas town, with little exposure to design, Brad got his first chance at decorating when he turned ten. His mother allowed both Brad and his brother to select the wallpaper for their bedrooms. The burgeoning decorator chose a psychedelic, overscaled, leather-belt-motif paper. The belts ran horizontally and vertically, forming a giant plaid pattern. "The best part was the gold metallic Mylar belt buckles," he recalls. "I remember thinking it was very modern." So enamored of the design, he even asked the wallpaper hanger to cover the ceiling. "It was pretty insane, but I loved it and I knew then I loved design." First he studied business and economics and built a small house for himself, a process that he treasured and enjoyed. A local designer suggested that he move to New York and formally learn the trade. Although Brad was "scared to death" and thought the idea was crazy, he followed the advice. After graduating from the Fashion Institute of Technology in design, he went to work for two luminaries. First, Jed Johnson, a designer whom

**DECORATIVE DETAILS** All of the possessions that I've collected throughout the years give my rooms soul. A lot of the things I accumulate are handmade—I love pottery and favor simple vignettes to showcase my organically shaped collections. Neutral tones and interesting textures also add softening layers that help relax any hard objects or edges, while making a room warm and inviting.

Brad describes as a man with great integrity and talent, and then the highly respected Thad Hayes. "I learned so much from both men and really honed my skills."

Twenty years later Brad is still impressed with fearless-ness, appreciates the unexpected, is enthralled by the process of design, and influenced by nature. "I wish I could say that it's all about the furniture, the artwork, or the things that fill a home but, honestly, I think it's the people and memories that ultimately make a house a home." Most Saturday nights you will find Brad at home, sitting in a large "perfectly worn" leather club chair, listening to music, having a cocktail, and taking in his surroundings. "It's usually at this moment that I don't have a care in the world. I think Charles Eames was right; we should take our pleasures seriously."

**MAKING AN ENTRANCE** Good lighting, a welcoming environment, and interesting objects are essential; these are the things that provide clues to the homeowner's life and personality. When I come home, I feel relaxed and content. Of course, I want others to have the same experience, but I also want them to know that they are in for a good time. A genuine welcome can only come from hosts that love their home, friends, and surroundings.

**FLOWERS AND FRAGRANCES** Whenever I am at home I burn Esteban Cedre incense; the warm and woody cedar scent is great. I love being outdoors and I am drawn to loose, natural arrangements made up of freshly cut flowers and big leafy greens. Living in the city, I don't have any type of outdoor garden, so candles and greenery help to bring a little bit of the outdoors into my apartment.

**A BEAUTIFUL BED** I keep the same linens on my bed year-round, although during the cold New York winters I do enjoy flannel sheets. I like a down feather mattress top between the fitted sheet and the mattress, covered with a simple blanket and a few decorative throw pillows. It's the easiest way to give the bed interest and it looks very inviting.

**ENTERTAINING THOUGHTS** Most of the time I will have a handful of people over and we gather around the coffee table with hors d'oeuvres and cocktails. It's always a casual affair, much less stressful than a dinner party, and it allows people to relax and feel at home. I load up a huge round tray with cheeses, grapes, crackers, salami, dips, vegetables, and olives. When guests arrive, I place the tray in the center of the table. I am then free for the rest of the night; all I have to worry about is making sure everyone has a fresh cocktail.

# KEN FULK
## FEAR OF EXPRESSION IS STYLE'S BIGGEST ENEMY.

"Anyone who lives within their means suffers from a lack of imagination." The immortal words of Oscar Wilde are emblazoned in gold across the window of a 1920s industrial building belonging to interior designer Ken Fulk. The former S&M leather factory, located in the SoMa (South of Market) district of San Francisco, is no ordinary place. Both a home and office, the lower floors of the sprawling building serve as a work space and a by-appointment-only house of curios. Above the studio and beyond a glass door marked "*Privé*" is the large open-loft living quarters. From top to bottom, the atelier is layered with interesting (and sometimes peculiar) objects: a chandelier made from weathered saw blades, a gallery of erotic art spanning the centuries, various forms of taxidermy, and softly focused photography by Robert Stivers are just a few of the curiosities. The uncompromising manner in which each object is carefully curated can be found in all of Ken's interiors and those of his clients.

A true sophisticate, Ken owns homes across the United States, including a ranch in Napa, California, and a New England Cape Cod cottage in Provincetown, Massachusetts. The self-professed "house junkie" considers his addiction the equivalent of a forced savings account and is endlessly hunting for his next fix. "I am forever in the midst of a love affair with one house or another, and I always have a possible mistress waiting in the wings." Currently, Ken has fallen "madly in love all over again" with the Napa ranch that he shares with his partner, Kurt Wootton, their three golden retrievers, and one fat cat. The ranch is simple, comfortable, rustic, and almost stark in comparison to his home and hectic life in San Francisco. A forty-five-foot-long pool, crisp white buildings, and wooden fence surrounding the property offer a sharp contrast to the rolling hills and ancient oaks in the distance. A submerged bench running the length of the pool is the perfect place to lounge and take in the scenery. The interiors of the house are white and black, with a few organic neutrals and the occasional punch of red. There is no cell reception, no TV, and no Internet. It is a place where Ken is happily forced to relax. Few things bring him greater joy than spending time in

**DECORATIVE DETAILS** Good lighting, music, laughter, books, photographs of family and friends, and trinkets collected from various travels all remind me of a life well lived. I hate it when great wine is missing from my home, and I will never forgo candlelight at night.

the wine country, unwinding with his partner, reading by a roaring fire, dreaming of a comfortable good night's sleep, taking a hot bath, and being surrounded by their beloved dogs. The four-legged children of this notorious "neat freak" add just the right amount of chaos to keep his "neuroses" in check.

When time allows, Ken flies east to spend time at their home in Massachusetts. It's a place where days are spent riding bikes, hiking to the beach, and socializing nonstop. The picturesque old New England house, accented with dormer windows and wide-planked sloping floors, is filled with odd treasures and kitschy art—objects that could easily look reckless in less artistic hands. "Creating a home should make you smile, it should never be boring, and always filled with things that you like. You can always change your mind and try something new."

**MAKING AN ENTRANCE** The first thing that I do when returning home is to stop and exhale. Behind the front door, I like to create a place where people can pause and decompress, if only for a moment. An entryway needs to be well appointed, no matter the size of a home. Everyone wants a spot to toss the keys, take off their shoes, and check the mirror.

**FLOWERS AND FRAGRANCES** With the exception of hydrangeas, I don't like blue and purple flowers; somehow they feel artificial. I gravitate toward white flowers and shades of green that look like the unripened color of spring. I am obsessed with the scent of peonies, lavender, roses, and the lingering smell of a fire long after it's been extinguished. In the winter, I love something woodsy and smoky with hints of leather and sandalwood. Diptyque's Feu de Bois or Le Labo's Cedre are two candles that fit the bill. In the summer, I prefer the crisp aroma of Ydra by Tocca. It's the perfect blend of Mediterranean fig and cucumber.

**A BEAUTIFUL BED** A good reading light and a window with a view are a must in the bedroom. As for the bed, I'm a big fan of McRoskey mattresses, and I love freshly ironed linens. A blanket of cotton, wool, or cashmere (depending on the season) is always on my bed. I also like to have a bed coverlet available; they are great for covering all your sins and make the bed look perfect until you have fresh sheets again.

**ENTERTAINING THOUGHTS** Inviting someone into your home is one of the most gracious and personal gestures you can extend. Late fall and winter are my favorite seasons for entertaining. As a kid, I always loved it when the time changed, the days got shorter, and I could peer into people's houses while walking home. It was magical to see the start of an evening, dinner being prepared, the table being set, and a fire being built. The purpose of entertaining is not to impress but to enjoy.

# STEVEN GAMBREL

## STYLE IS LIVING IN AUTHENTIC SURROUNDINGS
## THAT ALIGN WITH YOUR LIFESTYLE.

A passion for old houses, historic buildings, and community life brings together many Sag Harbor residents, including Steven Gambrel and his partner, John Chris Connor. The former whaling town, with its narrow streets and centuries-old homes, first attracted Steven during a winter break from the University of Virginia. The architecture major began dreaming of restoring a home in the picturesque Hamptons hamlet. After renting a cottage in the village, he and Chris were eager to make a purchase and renovate a place of their own. First, a boarding house, followed by a nineteenth-century property with a barn and pool house, then finally a one-acre estate discovered by their Labradoodle, Dash. "Dash wouldn't stop racing to the water at the edge of the overgrown lot. The house was a mess, but the view of the cove was amazing. It was the first time for me that nature won out over architecture," says Steven.

Widely known for his confident color combinations (rosy pinks, misty blues, deep amethysts) and bold sense of scale, Steven is always respectful of a home's architecture while keeping the interiors relevant and contemporary. "I like mixing many styles and elements, but they must be appropriate to the spirit of the home. I don't want my house to feel like it belongs to any time or place other than right now." His homes, which also include a townhouse in New York City's West Village, are prime examples of his ability to mix tradition with the here and now. Both residences are in historic districts that boast an early nineteenth-century village vibe, yet they are fresh in style and interpretation. "I don't like expectedness and I'm always a little let down by homes that betray an owner's passion."

His interests range from discussions about historical homes to the delights of sketching, reading,

**DECORATIVE DETAILS** The little details are so important. Personal style and the atmosphere you create come from a considered environment—music, dogs and people, fresh produce, home cooking, artful tablescapes, a fire in the fireplace, and very low lighting are key ingredients. Each detail in our homes is layered with extreme consideration and truly reflects our passions.

and travel. Many drawings from his notebooks often are the basis of his designs. The Flemish facades he sketched while in Brussels inspired a pair of twin head-boards in one of the guest rooms. "The past is what adds layers of patina and depth." Another must for the Virginia native is a bit of the unforeseen. A wooden block hallway, matching the facade of Mount Vernon, greets his enchanted guests to his country house, while salvaged marble floors from an outdoor sculpture garden at the Museum of Modern Art give the kitchen an interesting story. In the large living area, built within the walls of a 1964 garage, Steven designed a rug to perfectly align with the wide pine floor planks reclaimed from an eighteenth-century house in Maine.

The property also includes a charming guesthouse on the water's edge and a stone barn, designed in the spirit of a boathouse. It's a favorite spot for dinner parties and drinks by the fire. The parklike parcel of land, teeming with boxwood shrubs, locust trees, and gracious stone terraces, is the perfect year-round playground for friends and dogs alike.

**ENTERTAINING THOUGHTS** Summer in Sag Harbor is my favorite time to entertain at home, usually poolside. Meals are always given great deliberation, but nothing is overly fancy and dogs are always welcome. Often fresh local produce inspires our menu and we keep ingredients simple; the goal is to make entertaining look effortless. Off-season in the country is wonderfully quiet and makes for treasured intimate evenings with friends gathered by the fire. Both times of the year are charming in their own right.

**MAKING AN ENTRANCE** Low lighting and flickering candles not only illuminate the entryway but also add visual warmth and put visitors at ease. I like to create a welcoming atmosphere that offers my guests a sense of the unexpected; I want people to experience a bit of escape from the everyday. When I come home, I take a moment to look around. I am always curious about how things may have changed in my absence.

**FLOWERS AND FRAGRANCES** I am relatively consistent when it comes to flowers and scents at home. As for candles, I stay true to Diptyque's Baies; it's a classic. White peonies are my favorite flower, and I like flowering branches. I don't really care for strong flower colors as they tend to confuse the color story of the house, so I usually stick with white and green flowers.

**CREATURE COMFORTS** Nothing beats a bath or long shower, a great kitchen, healthy cooking, handsome rooms filled with familiar things, entertaining friends, music, reading, sunsets over the cove, and playing ball with Dash.

**A BEAUTIFUL BED** I never change my linens with the season. I always opt for crisp, ironed custom sheets, tucked in with a cotton blanket and a big down duvet folded at the foot of the bed. Long's Bedding on the Upper West Side has the best mattresses.

## BROOKE AND STEVE GIANNETTI
### WE FILL OUR HOME WITH THINGS THAT MAKE
### US HAPPY AND GIVE OUR LIFE MEANING.

While opposites may attract, Los Angeles–based architect Steve Giannetti and his wife, Brooke, an interior designer, make a strong case for partnering with someone who shares your values and understands your passions. The white Shingle-style Santa Monica cottage they built and share with their three children, two dogs, and several chickens is a testament to their interests and talents. Nothing in their home is too precious, and everything bears the marks of fascinating tales. But above all, it reflects their love of family life and their innate ingenuity. Both Brooke and Steve appreciate and respect homes that are well constructed and well considered. However, they prefer their rooms to be filled with slightly imperfect objects, gently worn furniture, and quirky items that tell a story.

Inspired by the coastal retreats of the 1910s that had been built for the residents of downtown Los Angeles, the Giannettis sought to construct a modern-day cottage with timeless appeal. Building an Old World–looking structure with twenty-first-century appliances and necessities was a top priority. The couple employed many clever tricks and ideas to achieve their shared goal. Salvaged antique doors in faded shades of pine and gray replaced standard stock items. Inexpensive drop cloths from Home Depot were used for drapery and to upholster furniture, adding instant antique appeal. "It's a great material that doesn't cost much and gets softer with

**ENTERTAINING THOUGHTS** A relaxed atmosphere and dining room that is conducive to a lively dinner party and good conversation is of the utmost importance. Our long farmhouse table promotes a casual environment and is especially great when you have children. We like to use a mélange of seating: benches, slipcovered chairs for easy cleaning, and masculine leather chairs that only get better with age. Summer is always a favorite time for entertaining. We open all of the doors to our garden, allowing for a wonderful, casual flow. Keeping things simple lets us enjoy the party, too.

each wash," says Brooke. When they recently remodeled a powder room, located near the back garden, they looked to nature for inspiration. An ornate marble planter became a perfect one-of-a-kind sink. And when they were unable to find the ideal waterspout, Brooke literally pulled one from the fountain outside the house. Such a unique style is admittedly born out of a desire to repurpose beautiful objects and create spaces with emotional impact.

No detail is overlooked in the Giannetti home. Eight-foot-long plank boards (in varying shades) nailed directly to plywood subflooring create exquisite flooring. A mixture of lighting calls to mind an earlier era; aged wall sconces, period ceiling lamps, and schoolhouse fixtures in the kitchen brighten each room and create natural warmth. Throughout the house, walls, trim, and ceilings are all painted in the same tones (Farrow & Ball being a favorite) to create a cocoonlike feeling. Everything is set against a backdrop of a calming and limited color palette of pale grays, muted taupes, natural linen, and subdued blues.

**A BEAUTIFUL BED** Our bedroom must have a calm color palette that creates a peaceful place to begin and end our day. We have fallen in love with the relaxed elegance of pure linen sheets in off-white. Incorporating interesting textures in neutral colors, such as soft cotton and matelassé, adds character to our room. Vintage velvet pillows in a pale blue or green add a touch of romance and softness to both the bed and space.

Never ones to hide flaws, the creative couple celebrate the patina of life that only comes with the passage of time. Pockmarked floors resulting from kids playing with toys, chipped paint from a wayward scooter, and a discolored kitchen counter from a tray of hot cookies baked by their daughter make Brooke and Steve smile. "Most people try to wipe stuff clean and keep everything perfect, but that's the beauty of personal things. They hold your memories," says Steve.

**MAKING AN ENTRANCE** In our entryway, we built a wall with lockers so that each family member has a place to store his or her belongings. There are hooks for the kids' backpacks, shelves for storage, and a place to charge phones. Seating is also important and makes the entry feel more like a welcoming room than a place you simply pass through when coming in the door. Everyone needs a spot to pull off a pair of rain boots or sit and wait for the kids.

**DECORATIVE DETAILS** Homes that don't incorporate cherished possessions turn us off both creatively and emotionally. All of the vintage and antique pieces that we have gathered at local flea markets or during our travels add much richness and fond recollections to our home. Our most charming treasures start with one piece that really intrigues us; it could be a vintage board game, vellum books, antique textiles, or a gorgeous piece of glassware. The result is a wonderful ensemble of objects that have meaning and memories.

**FLOWERS AND FRAGRANCES** We have a wonderful garden filled with roses, lavender, and rosemary. Living in California, we are fortunate that we can cut these fresh flowers and fill our house with their beauty and natural scent. During the winter months, when our garden is not in full bloom, we light Linnea's Lights candles. Their Winter candle is a clean, fresh fragrance scented with evergreen, mint, and cranberry—perfect for the holiday season. Roses are our favorite flower for both aroma and sight. Lavender is great as well, and it's not too feminine for our boys to enjoy.

**CREATURE COMFORTS** Our morning walks together give us physical energy to get through our long day as well as time to connect before parting ways. Time working in the garden is the perfect workout, both physically and emotionally for Brooke, while Steve finds painting at our weekend home to be emotionally rejuvenating. These are the moments when time seems to stand still.

# PHILIP GORRIVAN

## A HOUSE SHOULD BE AUTHENTIC, UNIQUE, AND REFLECT THE PERSONALITY OF ITS OWNER. THESE TRAITS ARE WHAT GIVE A HOME TRUE STYLE AND A SOUL.

Philip Gorrivan's Upper East Side prewar apartment is the perfect combination of continental style and 1930s New York glamour, with early-American heirlooms and art masterfully mixed in for good measure. Unique twists on historical yet updated elegance abound. Glamorous rooms full of abundant color offer tribute to some of his favorite places and designers. The dramatic black-and-white octagonal hallway pays homage to the lobby of the Carlyle Hotel as decorated by Dorothy Draper in 1930, while the black-mirrored kitchen backsplash was inspired by Yves Saint Laurent's Paris apartment. With just the right touch of grandeur, the apartment is still cozy and welcoming. More importantly, it is a family home. Antiques are tempered with comfortable upholstery and soft furnishings, creating a family-friendly environment for Philip, his wife, Lisa, their two children, and a fifty-pound standard poodle. "I believe that beautiful design and liveability can co-exist," says Philip.

Two limed oak tables and an upholstered banquette form a dining niche for entertaining, family dinners, and homework. A collection of drawings that spans three centuries covers the dove-gray lacquered walls, further defining the area. "I like spaces that are filled with layers, textures, and unexpected combinations creating an interesting narrative." Known for his inspirational and timeless approach, the New England native describes his style as modern preppy. "I grew up textbook preppy with a French Moroccan mother, so I take pleasure in a combination of influences."

For interiors, Philip uses a mix of periods and a dose of wit applied to things once typically traditional, which he achieves through color choices and fabrics. A perfect

**MAKING AN ENTRANCE** In theatrical terms, "making an entrance" means something that is attention grabbing or refers to a character entering a scene for the first time. It's the same idea when thinking about an entryway at home; it's a place that instantly sets the tone. Ours is a black lacquered, perfectly balanced, octagonal-shaped gallery with an inlaid marble slab floor and engravings from Sir William Hamilton's eighteenth-century book on antiquities adorning the walls. This place has a true thespian quality.

example is the Gorrivans' family room. Even though it is the smallest space in the apartment, this is where Philip, Lisa, and the children are happiest. The walls, custom-sectional sofa, and curtains are fully upholstered in one of Philip's fabrics and the ceiling is coffered and papered in a faux marquetry. "It's truly a cocoon of comfort for the whole family. The deep-red carpet and accents always make the blues go away."

When not at home in New York, the Gorrivans spend time at their house in Connecticut. Like their apartment, the 1840s cottage is a series of inviting rooms (on a smaller scale) with comfortable places to sit and enjoy the weekend. Art and family antiques fill the charming house. Summers are spent gardening, swimming, cooking, and entertaining friends. In winter months, there is cross-country skiing and dinners by the fire in the formal dining room. "My wife, Lisa, makes delicious veal stew and I enjoy roasting chicken with lots of fresh herbs and brussels sprouts. The house always smells so good when guests arrive."

**DECORATIVE DETAILS** Shiny is happy. Lacquered surfaces, whether on the wall, trim, or ceiling, is a favorite finishing detail. Other important particulars include layers of art, interesting objects, lots of books, plush rugs, custom wallpaper on the ceiling, and our poodle, Leo—the ultimate furry accessory.

**FLOWERS AND FRAGRANCES** Nothing is more gorgeous than fresh garden roses, especially the 'Yves Piaget' roses that I grow at our house in Connecticut. The slightly ruffled, lightly scented petals are otherworldly and infuse instant glamour to any room. As a general rule, I prefer pink and white flowers indoors and I tend to avoid strong colors and scents, with the exception of gardenias. The same holds true for room fragrance. I generally prefer room sprays to candles. With a spray you get the pure essence without the waxy undertones. Both Feu de Bois and Tubereuse by Diptyque are captivating scents.

**A BEAUTIFUL BED** I like a clean, tailored bed with crisp white percale sheets (accented with shades of gray), a pique blanket cover, a lightweight blanket, and a down duvet folded up at the end. It is essential to always use the best down pillows for the most comfort, and the same is true for the mattress. Monogrammed and embroidered pillows always add a personal touch. Other must-haves are blackout shades for sleeping, well-stocked side tables, and very soft carpeting.

**ENTERTAINING THOUGHTS** I like to entertain a large group in our intimate dining area. I strive for a mix of formality and informality in the table setting. We rarely serve plated dinners; it's just too formal, and I prefer a "family style" where everyone helps themselves. I always use place cards and thick linen napkins. Flower arrangements are kept low so as not to hinder conversations.

# NICKY HASLAM

## NEVER TRY TOO HARD. STYLE SHOULD MAKE YOU SMILE AND LIFT THE SPIRITS.

Nicky Haslam is a man who knows how to bring a room to life through fabulous furnishings and a charismatic personality. Creatively and emotionally, he is inspired by quick wit, fearlessness, beauty, interesting people, history, charm, and trivial details. "I am a mine of information about utterly useless facts," he proudly acknowledges. Growing up in a stately seventeenth-century manor house in rural Buckinghamshire, and confined to a bed at the age of seven as a result of polio, he became an astute observer of detail. After his recovery, he attended Eton and honed his talent for art, especially watercolor, and socializing. From the moment he left the prestigious school, he began a long and illustrious career of casting a spell on society and the design cognoscenti. The list of friends and fans is endless and as far-reaching as the Duchess of Windsor and Cole Porter to Kate Moss, Mick Jagger, Cecil Beaton, Bill Blass, Bryan Ferry, Andy Warhol, and Lady Diana Cooper.

Whether discussing people or interiors, Nicky is never short on words or opinions. "I don't like highly polished cheap floorboards, minimalism, or taking one's home too damn seriously. Serious people can be such bores, and serious interiors are even worse." In 1978, he acquired a lease through the National Trust on the Hunting Lodge that had once belonged to decorator John Fowler of the fabric house Colefax and Fowler. "When it went on the market, I thought every design queen in the world would put a bid on it, so I did nothing," he recalls. Months later, he learned that the historical Jacobean home was still available and he grabbed it the next day. It has been his primary residence ever since. For practical

**MAKING AN ENTRANCE** It's important that the entrance set the tone for the rest of the house. It should be enticing and not formidable; you should walk in and feel as if you are going to have a good time. When I come home, I am instantly at ease, as if a weight has been lifted off my shoulders. I want for others to experience the same feeling when they are invited into my home and trust that good thoughts will flood their mind. I certainly hope that they are delighted by the surroundings and not thinking about how to quickly find the loo.

purposes, Nicky divides his time between a London apartment where he "sleeps" and the Hunting Lodge, the place where he says he truly "lives."

He firmly believes that houses are meant for living and each room of his home reflects his eclectic style and colorful life. Corners brim with personal details, piles of books cover every surface, photo albums are neatly stacked under tables, and fresh flowers from the garden scent the air. He makes no secret that he thinks the pale-pink brick structure is quite possibly the most perfect dwelling in England and that the gardens are spectacularly pretty. These days he is happiest when playing gardener and learning to understand why, when, and how things grow. In warmer months, he opts for having a massage on the lawn and dining by candlelight on the terrace at night. To add visual interest, he prefers that the grass be mowed in a different pattern each week. Even in the silent dead of winter you are likely to find the budding horticulturist in his dressing gown, futzing in the garden, and dreaming up where to place a faux door for climbing clematis. Little surprise he thinks English decorator Nancy Lancaster had it right when she wrote, "To make a space look quiet you have to complicate everything."

**FLOWERS AND FRAGRANCES** I very rarely use artificial scents in a room and will always opt for natural aromas that radiate throughout the house with each season. Springtime breezes, autumnal bonfires, freshly cut summer grass, and log fires in the winter are simply the best. I gravitate toward English garden flowers that naturally soften a room (hyacinths, sweet peas, and roses). I am also partial to blowsy flowers like tulips and peonies. I like anything so long as it's pink, and the paler the better. In a pinch, white will work, but I really like pink. I'm not a huge admirer of garishly colored flowers.

**DECORATIVE DETAILS** Cachepots, jars of cigarettes, dogs, friends, soft sofas, log fires, flowers, photograph albums, books, books, and more books are what bring my home to life. I don't consciously collect anything that is too precious or impersonal. Likewise, I never buy anything purely for its value. I enjoy possessions that smile back at me. My favorite details are the little odd touches in my home and paintings by longtime friends, Graham Sutherland, David Hockney, and Lucian Freud.

**A BEAUTIFUL BED** I am hopeless when it comes to making beds. I just rely on beautiful sheets and pillows made for me by Gayle Warwick. I don't like cushions or throw pillows. Nothing is more annoying than having to remove extraneous pillows every time you want to nap. I do like down duvets, and in England electric blankets are a necessity. I will always want a dog, a telephone, and masses of books in my bedroom.

**CREATURE COMFORTS** I can't live without good friends, books, light rain, sun, fresh air, new places, new people, old people, old friends, the view down to the lake, and the autumn light. Reflecting on my past and focusing on the future has always been, and probably always will be, a favorite pastime.

**ENTERTAINING THOUGHTS** I'm a pretty good cook and I prefer to do everything myself. When I entertain, I like it to appear as casual as possible, but in fact I will have orchestrated everything quite carefully. I want to create sights, sounds, and tastes that will surprise the eye, mouth, and ear. Simple meals are the best, but remember that simplicity comes on two levels. A layer of caviar spread on steak tartare is simple. So, too, is scrambled eggs made with water (never cream) and served with *pain perdu*. Lady Diana Cooper had the best recipe for a great dinner party—have too much to drink and chocolate for dessert.

# ASHLEY HICKS

## I HAVE NO ILLUSIONS THAT MY TASTE IS IN ANY WAY BETTER THAN ANYONE ELSE'S; IT'S JUST DIFFERENT. IF IT'S NOT PERSONAL, IT'S NOT STYLE—IT'S AFFECTATION.

A series of old farm buildings with several small additions sit quietly amid a famously beautiful garden in rural Oxfordshire, England. The Grove's garden and main house was once home to the late, legendary designer David Hicks. It is still where his wife, Lady Pamela, resides. Their son, Ashley, now lives in the outbuildings when he is not working in London. While David's signature is everywhere outside, Ashley has made a distinctly individual mark within his own dwellings. Deep-green walls, which he hand-painted to imitate stitched leather, reveal one of his artistic talents. Each object that meets the eye is both striking and highly personalized. A portrait of David (sketched by his granddaughter Angelica) lives next to a lump of stone found in the adjoining field and a box decorated by his sister India Hicks. Many treasures lovingly sit atop cabinets designed and painted by Ashley.

An architect by training, he inherited his father's flair for artful compositions and distinctive interiors. Even as a young child, he designed military hardware with very "Hicks-like" graphics. "I share my father's passion for history, design, and beauty, but we are different in many ways," he admits. "I like subtlety and quiet effects, which were not his style." Ashley is happy to go against prescribed rules and eccentricity is in his nature. "I do slightly odd things like sculpting monkeys to decorate a twig-framed mirror made with my

**MAKING AN ENTRANCE** A hall table at the door is a must. It's essential to have somewhere to chuck keys and mail. For my country home, I designed a table with a steel base inspired by an African mask; for London, I made a faceted pink tabletop on a single, carved, and bronzed camel's leg. I like something unusual and unexpected—a surrealist statement, a bit of mystery.

daughter, Ambrosia." His regal, red bedroom showcases his natural whimsy and flamboyance. Bloodstain-red walls, resembling Aztec masonry, bear a portrait of a "robust-looking female ancestor" and watercolors of his parents by British artist Richard Chopping, whose paintings graced the covers of ten James Bond novels.

The solitude of home affords Ashley time to indulge his passions—working with his hands and reading Jonathan Franzen, Thomas Pynchon, and Anthony Trollope in the bath. Driven by his imagination, he is left cold by formulaic decorating and "hideous" design. Quick with an opinion, he passionately believes that idle fancy is the cornerstone of creativity. He also dislikes excessive educational material in museums, believing it blocks natural curiosity. When the designer is not dreaming up new projects or crafting furniture, fabric, and tiles, he retreats to his much-loved garden. Like his father, the soil and flowers offer a place of seclusion and inspiration. Equally, he adores many of the same roses that David cultivated, with one caveat, marbleized 'Variegata di Bologna', a variety his father "loathed." "Well, there we are," he smiles. "That's my favorite quote. I want it on my gravestone, in quotation marks. It suits just about every occasion."

**A BEAUTIFUL BED** My bloodred country bedroom is a retreat. I don't have a television, only beautiful things to gaze at before going to sleep and when I wake up. Perspex cases throughout the space are filled with old bits of gold, nothing valuable, but very beautiful. The effect is like sleeping in an Aztec tomb. I like a tailored bed, but I am also lazy. I solve that problem by using a simple bedspread embroidered with ribbon in an abstract design. I can pull it up or down and it does not need to be removed. When it comes to linens, I am easily pleased with all-white cotton sheets covering a firm mattress.

**ENTERTAINING THOUGHTS** I have to admit that I'm not the greatest host in the world. I am often called a hermit, but I do love June in the country. Nothing is better than seeing my marbleized faience d'Apt plates groaning with a very unsophisticated English country lunch of chicken and roast potatoes cooked by my marvelous factotum, John Weiland. I always give garden tours to anyone who shows the slightest interest, regaling them with stories of my father's eccentric ways.

**FLOWERS AND FRAGRANCES** I love the smells of wood smoke in winter and fresh roses in summer. If I'm lucky and one of my treasured tuberoses bloom in the greenhouse, I rush it indoors; it is the most exquisite scent of all. I'm not a born gardener, unlike my father, but I love my garden and cannot abide sterile, store-bought flowers. Instead, I grow my own: hellebores in the winter (black, gray, pink, and maroon); tulips in the spring; peonies, roses, and poppies in the summer; and dahlias (which my father detested) in the autumn.

**DECORATIVE DETAILS** Details are important in every room, even the bathroom. My bathtub's backsplash is a glass-covered wall decorated with Giambattista Nolli's 1748 map of Rome. The date of the print appears in raised roman numerals on the tub's panel. As a rule, I generally display art by my friends and family. My children's drawings and paintings are everywhere; I was very amused when an esteemed decorating magazine removed most of their art for a photo shoot. My outraged teenage daughter sent me a beautiful drawing with the inscription "I hope this Child Art will be deemed unsuitable for magazines." A signature detail is my sculpted cast-bronze handles for cabinetry.

# INDIA HICKS

## STYLE IS UNDERSTANDING WHO YOU ARE AND KNOWING HOW TO SAY IT IN YOUR OWN LANGUAGE.

"It was love at first sight," says India Hicks, recalling her earliest encounter with Hibiscus Hill, the Harbour Island house that she shares with her husband, David Flint Wood, their four children, three dogs, one cat, and a "bad-tempered" parrot. Set on a sand dune and three acres of rolling gardens, with sweeping views of the Sargasso Sea, India decided to buy the plantation-style house before she even stepped foot in the door. The charming residence has clearly evolved over time, layer upon layer, eschewing all pretension. Large plank floors once stained the shade of dark oak welcome bare feet each day. A perpetual sanding, from children and dogs fresh from the beach, gives the fir floors an aged patina that can only come from living on an island. "Our home is a storehouse of family history, a living archive that holds the treasures of our personal life," India affirms. "It speaks volumes of where we've been, who we are, and the distinctive style cultivated by our journey together."

India possesses a curious mind and instinctively finds imaginative ways in which to weave all that she loves into her life and home. Traditional European antiques harmonize effortlessly with a bright pink sofa, bookcases filled with keepsakes, and Caribbean influences. Intense hues of color, palm fronds, and seashells casually decorate each room. Once you know India, it comes as no surprise that she sees her life as a combination of "classic British taste with all the eccentricities" and traditional flavors of the island. "I now cannot live without uninterrupted runs on a three-mile stretch of sandy pink beaches or the sound of happy crickets at night."

Though raised by prominent parents—renowned interior designer David Hicks and Lady Pamela Hicks—India has carved out a colorful life all her own. "I am happy to no

**DECORATIVE DETAILS** I was seven years old when I asked my father to write in my little autograph book. "Good taste and design are by no means dependent upon money," he flamboyantly wrote. I think of his words almost daily, while trying to keep a sense of humor. Toy guns and Barbies decorate our garden lawn and three plastic goldfish (meant for the children's bath) are perfectly displayed in a Perspex case. I love big bowls of tropical fruit and pineapples on our dining table. Shocks of color and references to the Caribbean are everywhere.

longer be the daughter of, the granddaughter of, or the goddaughter to
someone. I am happy to finally be recognized as a mother, a model, and a designer. Really, just someone who is living
a life less ordinary." Perhaps it is why she
is happiest in the kitchen, surrounded by
the daily chaos of children, the smell of
something baking, an oversized wooden
fruit bowl filled with locally grown wa-
termelons, and her beloved dogs underfoot. A life less ordinary seems to suit
India Hicks extraordinarily well.

**CREATURE COMFORTS** The lush
landscape surrounding our home, as well as
our beloved pets, contributes to my comfort
and well-being. The house is situated above
three acres of rolling gardens that stretch
inland from the top of the dunes with
jungle on both sides and a valley of coconut
palms. We can watch the setting sun over
the distant rooftops. It's a magical moment
when the tropical night sky shines so bright
that you can see your shadow.

**FLOWERS AND FRAGRANCES** Tropical flowers don't last long after they're cut, so I am always cutting oversized palm fronds for the sitting room, kitchen, entrance hall, and bedrooms. Our rooms now look undressed without them. Thankfully, palm fronds last and are not in short supply. While I love the smell of the night-blooming jasmine that grows along our terrace, I miss having four seasons. I gravitate toward Christmassy smells all year. Perhaps it's just out of nostalgia. Christmas is when my mother comes to stay for a month.

**A BEAUTIFUL BED** A Lord Mountbatten Tester Bed dominates our room. I explained to the company I was Lord Mountbatten's granddaughter, trying to engineer a free sample, but they were not the least bit interested. My only bedding requirement is crisp white sheets free from dog hair. Two old-fashioned bolsters give our pillows a sense of order, and a superfluous duvet folded at the bottom of the bed completes the look.

**ENTERTAINING THOUGHTS** One of the great pleasures of living in a warm climate is eating outside. Whenever possible I set up breakfast, lunch, and dinner in the garden courtyard or on the beach. For the past decade, our cook, Claire, has been in charge of the meals. If Claire does not like the manners or morals of a visiting guest, it's unlikely they are invited back. She is "da Boss" as they say around here. We eat a lot of the locally made conch salad, which is thought to be an aphrodisiac. Perhaps that explains our four children.

**MAKING AN ENTRANCE** Palm fronds, shells, shark jaws, local straw, and India Hicks Crabtree & Evelyn candles are the first things that greet guests. Each item captures the essence of the island. You will also encounter a nasty wooden console that we inherited with the house and couldn't afford to change out. With time, children, and the demands of daily life, the table remains in the house. Actually, in thinking about it, I am annoyed that that console is still in my entryway.

# ERIC HUGHES AND NATHAN TURNER

## GREAT STYLE IS LIKE PORNOGRAPHY. I'M NOT SURE WE CAN DEFINE IT, BUT WE CERTAINLY KNOW IT WHEN WE SEE IT.

Malibu. The name alone conjures up warm, sandy beaches and miles of scenic beauty. Despite humble beginnings in the late 1920s, the famous locale is now synonymous with Hollywood royalty and fantastic architecture. To establish Malibu as a desirable location, studio carpenters were brought in to build cottages on thirty-foot ocean lots. The weekend retreats were then leased to silent film stars. By the end of the 1930s, 140 homes dotted the spectacular coastline.

The unassuming white clapboard home of interior designers Eric Hughes and Nathan Turner was originally built for film producer Frank Borzage, one of the first to be nominated for the Academy Award for Best Picture (then called Best Picture Production). Like the exterior, the white interiors are set against a largely restrained background. Slipcovered seating, quirky art, a collection of framed maps, flea-market finds, and an expansive view of the Pacific Ocean create a tranquil and serene weekend retreat. Ocean breezes waft in through open doors and windows. "The interiors are very white and simple. Nothing detracts from the incredible view," says Nathan.

Malibu befits the two talented men. Eric, a former film studio executive, has become a much-sought-after interior designer. His client list includes Sarah Jessica Parker, Michael Douglas and Catherine Zeta-Jones, and Kate Winslet. Nathan too boasts an impressive roster of celebrity clients. But don't let their lofty resumes fool you; both men possess a healthy dose of laid-back California charm. Their easygoing personalities naturally spill over to their life and home.

Personal belongings take precedence, as do rooms that can accommodate sandy feet, wet bathing suits, and lots of people. Rattan and wishbone-style chairs sport deep, comfortable cushions in cheerful shades of persimmon. Towels, straw hats, dog leashes, and carved wooden fish cling to a line of peg hooks. A large suspended lamp, made of wicker and braided rope, illuminates a pin board filled

**MAKING AN ENTRANCE** Our dogs and a long row of wood peg hooks that hold towels, hats, wetsuits, and swim trunks greet our guests. The wall of hooks is really practical and decorative, too. Above the pegs are framed maps from beach and island vacations. The last time we drove from San Diego to Cabo San Lucas, Eric picked up the map of Baja, California, from the gas station.

with special memorabilia and photos. "The corkboard is my favorite object in the room," says Eric. "It holds many cherished memories."

Weekends in Malibu revolve around friends, family, and food. Nathan, an accomplished cook, is happiest in the green lacquered kitchen with his permanent audience, Daisy and Nacho, their yellow and black Labradors. Dinners are served outside and are always simple—grilled sea bass, roasted corn, heirloom tomatoes, and fresh peaches are part of the repertoire. A side deck functions as an outdoor dining room, which is perfect for lounging and morning coffee. When the weather does not agree, a table designed by Eric, made from an old marine chain, doubles as an indoor dining table and a whimsical place for lingering conversations.

**DECORATIVE DETAILS** Our entire house is paneled and painted in Benjamin Moore Super White; it gives the whole space a fresh, beachy feel. Inspired by the ocean, we used touches of striped fabrics, boating memorabilia, and a classic palette of red, white, and blue. The American flag photograph entitled *Underwater* by Oberto Gili is a playful piece that hangs about the dining table and embodies the spirit of our home.

**FLOWERS AND FRAGRANCES** In Malibu, we prefer the natural smell of fresh ocean breezes. There is always a door or window left open to let the scent in. Often we use palm fronds, sea grass, and large elephant ears in place of traditional flowers. Not only do they look natural in a seaside setting, but they also last forever. If we do use flowers, it is usually something simple, like ranunculus, tulips, or anemones in bright shades of purple, red, and orange.

**A BEAUTIFUL BED** We keep our bed super simple, but we never skimp on great linens and a good mattress. Clean, crisp lightweight cotton bedding dried in the sun is heavenly. Our seasons are so mild that there is no need to change the weight of our sheets. It's always a lightweight down cotton comforter (with no top sheet) and orderly pillows. Leontine Linens is our very favorite, both for clients and ourselves.

**ENTERTAINING THOUGHTS** Our entertaining style is very relaxed, never fussy, and almost always outside. Fresh food from the market is served family style. We select a menu and table setting in advance of our parties. The point of entertaining is to have fun, not spend the day in the kitchen or fussing over flowers. If it's in the budget, we will hire someone to help. It makes a huge difference when you are tired and it's time to clean up.

## KATHRYN M. IRELAND
### STYLE IS AN HONEST REPRESENTATION OF YOUR LIKES AND DISLIKES. IT'S THE SUM TOTAL OF WHO YOU ARE AND WHERE YOU'VE BEEN.

"Bohemian" is a word often used to describe the joyously unrestrained and exuberant Kathryn Ireland. Few other words better depict Kathryn's personality. Known for her relaxed style and fearless use of color and patterns, she decorates without regard for conventional rules and practices. In her own homes and those of clients, she skillfully mixes flea-market finds with noteworthy antiques to create eclectically comfortable rooms. The end result is magnificent houses lacking in pretentious grandeur. Her secret is layers and layers of color, texture, and pattern. "But here is the real trick," she says. "Never opt for matchy-matchy. Trust me, if you think it doesn't go together, then it goes."

Both her eighteenth-century farmhouse in the Tarn-et-Garonne region of the southwest of France (part of the Midi-Pyrénées) and a 1920s Spanish Colonial Revival home in Santa Monica are classic examples of her relaxed, congenial approach to living. Her life and style are all about comfort, and she is completely at ease with chipped china and nicked furniture. "Imperfection is part of life. Less than perfect things tell a story and make people feel comfortable." She is happiest when her homes are filled with friends, family, food, laughter, and a well-stocked drinks table. British by birth and raised in Scotland, Kathryn knows precisely how to blend the "English manor style" with healthy doses of California casual, no matter the continent or location.

**FLOWERS AND FRAGRANCES** My house almost always smells like fresh produce and flowers. I don't like candles with a cloying smell or anorexic-looking flowers. It seems that every magazine has a thing for phalaenopsis orchids. Yes, they have presence, they have height, they're durable, and the blooms literally last for months, but they are no longer unique. Life's ephemeral and cut flowers die, I get that. That's why they're a luxury and that's why I appreciate them all the more. There's something carpe diem–esque about an arrangement with a short life span. I like my flower arrangements to look messy and dishabille, like an unmade bed. I prefer old English roses for their scent and peonies for their voluptuousness.

Believing necessity is the mother of invention, Kathryn has her own innovative way of getting things done. If a favorite fabric has not had time to properly fade or age with sunshine and time, she takes matters into her own hands. She loves to wash things, hang them on the line, and let Mother Nature do the work. In fact, she was both shocked and appalled when she first moved from England to sunny Los Angeles and discovered that everyone had clothes dryers. "It's a sunny climate for God sakes!" She makes no secret that she prefers objects that are personal, dislikes perfectly creased pillows, and never wants a guest to wonder for a minute where they should sit or be relegated to uncomfortable chairs just because they work with a room. "Let's face it; a chair should be comfortable. It's designed for your rear end!" She is right, of course, but few people can pull off her unorthodox approach to design so exactingly, with such irreverent charm. "We Brits are just used to old, crumbling houses and water stains." And, Kathryn would argue, such an atmosphere provides a great juxtaposition when hanging an oversized photograph by Oberto Gili on a less-than-perfect wall. If we could all learn to adopt a laissez-faire approach, overlook imperfection, and layer in color, texture, and patterns that don't match, we would see that Kathryn is right—it all marries incredibly well.

**ENTERTAINING THOUGHTS** My favorite way to entertain is casually, last-minute, and preferably outdoors. The one thing I have learned is that you should never underestimate how much people eat, and make sure that you always have more than you need. I always have things in the fridge that I can pull out at the last minute—foie gras, olives, grapes, cheese, wine. I'm a great one for snacking. Thankfully farmer's markets are abundant in France. In California you can't leave your house without tripping over markets filled with stalls of artisanal *pico de gallo*, salsas, and relishes. I buy it all, especially tortilla chips in every color of corn—they look great on the table.

**MAKING AN ENTRANCE** When someone enters my home, I want them to feel an irresistible sense of comfort. The entryway immediately sets the mood; it is almost like the opening line of your autobiography. An enormous, formulaic foyer is the epitome of anticozy. This is one of the reasons I much prefer the Spanish motto *mi casa es tu casa* (my house is your house) as opposed to the stuffy French *pelouse interdite* (stay off the lawn).

**DECORATIVE DETAILS** My family, my photographs, my children's pottery and artwork, the books I've collected, the fabrics I've designed, and bits of flotsam and jetsam collected on my travels are at the heart and soul of my home. Furnishings and objects that are clearly touched and used give rooms a life. Everyone should take a few minutes to light a candle, dim the lights, and create some atmosphere.

**A BEAUTIFUL BED** My bed must have an array of patterns, color, two large back pillows, and a bolster. I don't like to "over-pillow" a bed, and yet, nothing looks worse than too few pillows. I want my pillows to look like a dog has just laid on them, nothing too perfect. I use white linens all year long and never change my linens with the seasons. That's a high standard I don't need in my life. Just give me Irish linen or 400-count percale cotton sheets, a duvet, a bedspread, and fresh air from an open window and I'm in heaven.

**CREATURE COMFORTS** Interaction with great clients and great friends is essential to my life. So, too, is seeing my children grow up and thrive. Cashmere, a great book, reading in bed, paddleboarding, and lying horizontally in the sun rank right up at the top of my list. Traveling and exploring turn me on spiritually, and I adore communing with nature, hiking in Topanga, and the quiet scent of sage.

# JAY JEFFERS
## STYLISH LIVING IS COMPLETELY SUBJECTIVE.

Wit and sophistication happily dwell within the walls of Jay Jeffers and his husband Michael Purdy's enchanting 1908 Edwardian cottage in San Francisco's Castro district. Very much a study in playful luxe, this vibrant home has been Jay's design laboratory for more than a decade. Lauded for his confident mixing of bold colors and playful fabrics, he knows how to inject interest and drama while creatively straddling the casual-versus-formal line.

Pale cinnabar living room walls, punctuated with gray crown moldings, bold stripes, antiques, and contemporary furnishings confidently suggest that this is no ordinary residence. The dining room walls are adorned with a diverse collection of oil paintings and portraiture that mix the new with the old, the quirky with the traditional, and the provocative with the serene. The work of several well-known artists including Forrest Williams, Sheldon Berkowitz, Christopher Brown, and local San Francisco talent Ada Sadler round out the eclectic mix. Beyond bold colors and pretty patterns, Jay plays with proportion and scale to create visual excitement, but more importantly, he knows exactly when to pull back. "If you don't have the right scale, it doesn't matter what you've done to the room or how much money you've spent—it is a failure." Each room is emblematic of Jay's ability to mix styles and periods. Aesthetically, he wants a space to feel as though it has been around for many years, a look he achieves by merging personal objects with traditional and contemporary pieces with touches of nostalgia and family heirlooms.

Though he chose a more indirect professional route (first a degree in international business and marketing), the Dallas native began perfecting his craft at the age of twelve, reading *Architectural Digest* and then regularly rearranging his room. "There

**DECORATIVE DETAILS** A house replete with furniture is just a house. A home, on the other hand, is a living, breathing entity full of personal treasures that change and evolve. My home is not large, but the living room, dining room, and kitchen combine to create a great space filled with favorite objects that make me smile. I know it sounds like a California thing, but I firmly believe that happy homes foster happy people.

were only four walls and about five pieces of furniture, but I explored every possible combination." While in design school, Jay discovered a vintage book by the legendary designer Billy Baldwin, a tome that shaped many of his ideas and opinions. "Paraphrasing Mr. Baldwin, 'If someone walks into a house and immediately says Billy Baldwin did this home, then I haven't done my job.' At the end of the day, interiors should reflect the inhabitants and embody their personal point of view." There is no telltale sign of a Jay Jeffers' room—the subtle clues lie in the thoughtfully edited objects.

Discriminating touches and elements of surprise abound—a boldly striped carpet runs down the stairs, a screen print of a bright pink Abraham Lincoln by Natalie Ammirato hangs against graphic Studio Printworks wallpaper, dimmers control every switch, and lightly scented candles burn in every room (except in the kitchen, which should only have the aroma of "a slow-cooking beef bourguignon").

**MAKING AN ENTRANCE** No matter the shape or size, an entry hall is like an opening act; you want to be subtle in your delivery, but enticing enough to make people want more. An interesting piece of furniture, a beautiful piece of art, and a scented candle immediately excite the senses.

**FLOWERS AND FRAGRANCES** I like scents that are clean and pure. My absolute favorite scent in the whole world is Hotel Costes candles and room sprays. It takes me back to a very happy time and place. Other favorites are lavender and fig. I stick with these fragrances and don't typically sway. I'm not much for scented flowers but I love peonies for their sight and subtle scent. Sadly, they are at their most beautiful just moments before their death, when the petals begin falling off the stems.

**A BEAUTIFUL BED** The big, puffy duvet look is not my thing. I like a clean and tailored bed with just a few accent pillows. I want a bed that looks beautiful when made and is easy to make back up after it's mussed. A medium-density firm mattress, crisp cotton sheets, a thin cashmere blanket, and a tailored blanket cover suit my tastes perfectly. Bedrooms should always feel calm and restful.

**ENTERTAINING THOUGHTS** Large parties aren't intimate enough for my liking. I need to connect with guests and talk with friends that I haven't seen in ages. Great people, easy drinks, good food, and a beautiful environment are key. I love cooking and prefer food that is local and in season. If I can't do it myself, there is a fabulous artisan pizza joint in San Francisco called Pauline's Pizza that sells half-cooked pizza. You take it home and reheat it for ten minutes. Add a fantastic salad and a really good wine and you're done.

# CELERIE KEMBLE
## AESTHETIC CHOICES ARE LIKE MUSICAL NOTES;
## STYLE IS WHEN THEY COME TOGETHER IN PERFECT HARMONY.

There is nothing typical about interior designer Celerie Kemble. Both her name and upbringing are wonderfully uncommon. The daughter of noted Palm Beach decorator Mimi Maddock McMakin, Celerie learned from an early age that individuality was more interesting than following a prescribed set of rules. After a few older ladies drinking Bloody Marys with celery stalks discouraged a pregnant Mimi from choosing an unordinary name for her daughter, she focused on the celery and contrarily selected the unique name. Growing up in a converted one-hundred-year-old historic church also contributed to Celerie's free spirit and inimitable point of view. "My mother has always been irreverent in her decisions, especially decorating. I learned my design vocabulary from her at a young age."

The home she now shares with her husband, Boykin Curry, and their three children, Rascal, Zinnia, and Wick, is equally out of the ordinary. Perched twenty-seven floors above Central Park, the large apartment with a private outdoor garden was once a hotel. And while the designer insists there is no great story to be told architecturally, the interiors tell another tale. Two samurai statues dressed in intricate eighteenth-century costumes stand at attention in the dining room, while a large stuffed peacock, called F. Bronson Van Cock, in honor of her best friend, renowned events

**ENTERTAINING THOUGHTS** When we have houseguests, we encourage them to enjoy one night out and one evening where we serve a casual dinner at home family style. Always think about your company and their needs. It is hard (and boring) to be an entirely passive guest. People like to serve themselves drinks, so keep the wine on the table or a bar in reach. I never seat my guests girl-boy-girl-boy; I seat them next to the partners I think they would most enjoy. If in a pinch, remember that wine, cheese, and a good laugh is all anyone really wants anyway.

designer Bronson Van Wyck, watches over the living room. She is not one to take decorating her home over seriously, nor does Celerie worry about the "stains of life" or broken objects. "I don't want to be a miserable casualty of the inevitable. In my own home, I am interested in personal style, comfort, and fun—not perfection."

Amber-colored grass-cloth wallpaper wraps around the large living space, offering a perfect surface for the notorious "redecorator." "The beauty of grass cloth is that it hides the holes left by the many nails that I have hammered." Celerie's walls are a changing gallery of oil paintings, old board games, photographs, children's artwork, and various odd objects. A long hallway lined in framed vintage party hats (many found on eBay), provide color, interest, and whimsy for both kids and adults. Linen, sea grass, Lucite, lacquer, and silk velvet are textural elements she can't get enough of; they pepper each room in her home. However, it is the myriad of materials and sentimental belongings that give her interiors interest and tell a story. Celerie is easily attached to special objects and not one to throw stuff

out and start anew. "I sometimes fear that my home may be more defined by what I hoard than what I edit."

The Harvard-educated Kemble dislikes pretention and craves cheerfulness in every room she designs, always more concerned that the space feels delightful rather than impressive. Likewise, acutely aware of the pleasure derived from her own thoughtfully considered childhood home, and how much it added to the family's sense of connectedness and identity, she gives equal care to the environment in which she is raising her own family. Her children take top priority, and she is happiest anywhere there is a sleeping child in her lap. "Like Charlotte Brontë, I'd rather be happy than dignified."

**MAKING AN ENTRANCE** It is easy to say that your entry should set the tone of your house, but it's true. Your home tells the story of your life and the entryway is your opening page. I have small children and I'm very sentimental, so I want my entrance to be friendly, irreverent (that is to say informal), and inviting. It should be clear that our home belongs as much to my children as to my husband and me.

**DECORATIVE DETAILS** I am drawn to things that are old, worn, and don't match, and where continuity comes from the love of the owner. I get very attached to things, which is part of the reason much of the furniture in my collection is replicated from pieces I bought years ago and I just couldn't get rid of no matter how hard I tried.

**FLOWERS AND FRAGRANCES** Many of my favorite smells are ones that remind me of growing up in Palm Beach—grapefruit, tuberose, jasmine, and gardenia. My all-time favorite fragrance is Jo Malone's Orange Blossom. I like a floral scent in my bedroom and a citrus one in my bathroom; everywhere else is selected by my mood and what I can find on hand. I love thistles, dahlias, fiddlehead ferns, belles of Ireland, delphinium, peonies, anemones, and ranunculus. If I ever start persecuting any specific flower, just knock me out.

**A BEAUTIFUL BED** I sleep on pure down pillows and appliquéd or embroidered bedding over the faintest of cream-colored Egyptian cotton sheets, preferably sateen. I'm monogamous when it comes to bed linens and not one to change my sheets with the seasons. My bedding is another skin and I like to buy several identical sets—just no top sheet, please. Bedding aside, a good book and notebook next to the bed, an easy-to-grab bathrobe or cashmere blanket, soft pillows, and a place for someone to sit other than on the bed spells perfection.

**CREATURE COMFORTS** I feel physically well when I have comfortable shoes, plenty of light, a view of the horizon, time to take a bath, sleep or snuggle, and space on the floor to roll around and stretch my back. I like to surround myself with people who don't take themselves too seriously.

# MALCOLM JAMES KUTNER

STYLISH LIVING IS HAVING A RELENTLESS SENSE OF CURIOSITY
AND A SPIRIT OF ADVENTURE ABOUT ALL THINGS.

For interior designer Malcolm James Kutner, home is about creating a sense of place. The native Houstonian has lived in many locales as diverse as Bali, Barcelona, Guatemala, London, Key West, and New York City. He has owned and rented both historic properties and modern spaces, where he has always endeavored to fashion calm and appropriate interiors. "I have come to understand that home is a shifting concept and an evolving emotional response. However, it must always nurture the marriage of suitability and beauty." His approach to design is accordingly neither strictly modern nor classically traditional but somewhere in between; it is an eclectic, worldly style that in the wrong hands could leave a room feeling disunited. However, just as wanderlust is at the core of his being, warmth, openness, and curiosity are in his DNA. These traits are visibly reflected in his 1920s Manhattan apartment.

His affinity for adventure and appreciation for unusual objects are revealed the moment you step into his world. Cork-lined entryway walls and a hand-painted floor of black and white diamonds pull you into this intriguing space. Moroccan carpets, temple bells from Cambodia, boxes from Botswana, and ancient currency from Mali all await discovery. Malcolm often reorganizes these tokens from his travels, artfully displaying them atop tables, bookshelves, or on the floor. However, he insists that a sense of humor is fundamental to a comfortable interior. "Playfulness is essential; it is important for me to not take all of this too seriously." A textbook example is an axe from Peter Buchanan-Smith's Best Made Company, which leans casually in a corner of the foyer.

When it comes to design, Malcolm sets out to tell a story and create a feeling rather than produce a look. His own home is no exception, nor is it a coincidence that his color palette is inspired by nature—a chief source of inspiration in all of his work. Complex hues of earthy browns, stormy grays, greens, blues, and golds reference some of his favorite landscape nuances, creating a peaceful refuge in the middle of a noisy city.

The late decorator William Pahlmann is high on Malcolm's list of favorite decorators and unquestionably inspired his richly colored living room, which is wrapped entirely in Donald Kaufman gunmetal gray, similar to Pahlmann's own 1940s New York living room.

**CREATURE COMFORTS** I take great comfort in such simple things as a good night's sleep, a delicious meal shared with friends, writing notes on engraved stationery, playing with dogs, falling asleep while reading on the sofa, curling up in a favorite chair, and having a long phone conversation with an old friend.

The masculine master bedroom is another study in the balance of periods, color, and texture. Midnight-blue walls, and midcentury eggplant-lacquered nightstands could look heavy and cold if not properly tempered with soft touches. To relax the space, a beaded panel from Thailand hangs over the raw silk curtains, monogrammed Leontine Linens grace the bed, and a sheared mink throw further softens the hard edges.

It's not one detail, or even several, that bring the apartment to life. It is the measured synthesis of a myriad of details. "I always want to be surrounded by the memories, possibilities, and irony of my life. In the words of Wallace Stevens, 'I am what is around me.'"

**FLOWERS AND FRAGRANCES** My first choice is the potpourri from Farmaceutica Santa Maria Novella. My favorite candles are Cire Trudon, especially the tobacco and leather scent of Ernesto. In warmer months, the smell of spearmint mixed with cloves in Abd el Kader is perfect. For flowers, I almost always prefer a single flower to a mixed arrangement. I think it's too easy for flowers to steal the show.

**MAKING AN ENTRANCE** I am a big believer in the entrance as the thesis statement of one's home. I like to think of the foyer as a sort of summary of the rest of my apartment. My foyer is, accordingly, replete with textures and objects that reflect the refuge, safety, and eclecticism that unfolds beyond.

**A BEAUTIFUL BED** Although it may not seem beautiful, a good mattress is a must; preferably no more than ten inches thick. I find eight inches to be the perfect height. I loathe those extrathick, extrapadded mattresses. I have a deep appreciation for bespoke products, which is one of the main reasons that I like Savoir Beds. To set the perfect bed, I use a fitted sheet and then sandwich a lightweight wool blanket between two flat sheets so the wool never touches the skin. I prefer a blanket

cover to a duvet, and I am no stranger to Leontine Linens or monograms. For a touch of humor, I made a Texas flag pillow from scraps of Fortuny. Percale sheeting from Sferra or Pratesi is always a favorite.

**ENTERTAINING THOUGHTS** I love to cook but I almost never do in New York City. Mostly, I take friends out for dinner, usually opting for somewhere familiar where I know the food and the ambiance will please my guests. When I do entertain at home, I will mix things up. It could be meatloaf on a cool summer night or fresh grilled fish and roasted vegetables in the winter. It gives your guests a break from the expected, provokes memories of a season just passed, or kindles anticipation for the seasons soon to come. As long as the food is fresh and simple, you can't go wrong.

## JOE LUCAS AND DAVID HEIKKA

### TO LIVE STYLISHLY YOU MUST INJECT IMAGINATION AND INDIVIDUALITY INTO EVERYDAY LIFE.

In the shadows of the Sunset Strip and celebrated Chateau Marmont hotel lies West Hollywood. Located between Hollywood and Beverly Hills, the historic district is full of architectural gems dating from the 1920s and 1930s. As movie studios moved into the area, it became a fashionable playground for celebrities, with many distinctive apartments, houses, and hotels being built. Along a shaded street, a charming 1920s French Normandy–style duplex, originally built for actor Lon Chaney, is now home to interior designer Joe Lucas and his partner, David Heikka.

A narrow walkway leads from a grassy front yard up to an external staircase turret and an ornate wooden door that opens directly onto a barrel-vaulted living room. Hardwood floors, stained-glass windows, and arched doorways are elements of the architectural vocabulary of this period. Joe, part owner of Harbinger and Lucas Studio, and David, who manages store design for a global company, share a sense of style that is rooted in tradition with occasional

**DECORATIVE DETAILS** Our home is an expression of our personalities. The bold wallpaper in our dining room, the dark moody walls of our bedroom mixed with cheerful shades of yellow, and our eclectic art collection reveal much about us. The details that imbue our rooms with soul include photographs, personal mementos, books written by friends, and furniture that has moved with us over the years.

bohemian flourishes. Both love a mix of objects that make them smile, especially abstract sculptures, quirky vintage paintings, and collections of pottery. However, as with many partnerships, their execution differs slightly. David prefers a clean and quiet aesthetic, while Joe likes a more layered effect, using color and lots of pattern. On the whole, both men crave comfortable surroundings and objects that are functional and personal; they also agree that everything in a room should not be shoved up against a wall. "Otherwise it's boring and looks like a middle-school dance where the boys are on one side of the room and the girls are on the other," says Joe.

Entertaining is another of the couple's shared passions, and Thanksgiving affords them the opportunity to splurge. Joe's turkey dinners are legendary, traditional, and large. On the first Thanksgiving in their current home, Joe and David hosted twenty-eight people, only four days after becoming residents. Accordingly, the bright dining room is one of their favorite rooms in the house. Walls are wrapped in bold herringbone stripe wallpaper designed by Idarica Gazzoni. The washed-out blue and dusty-lavender colorway is a perfect contrast to the high-gloss deep-purple ceiling and black trim and molding. A large Swedish mirror reflects colorful art and visually increases the size of the room. However, the pièce de résistance is an often-used antique English dining table. When the weather is warm (which is often), parties are moved outside to the back garden, a rare luxury in the neighborhood.

**ENTERTAINING THOUGHTS** Anytime of the year is a good time to entertain. Three things you can never have enough of are food, booze, and ice. For easy entertaining, we order Chinese food, serve Mount Gay rum, tonic, and a slice of lime, and play a rousing game of Bananagrams. David was a sixth grade spelling bee champion and is disarmingly competitive at board games (or any game, for that matter).

**FLOWERS AND FRAGRANCES** We're not big on too many fragrances and would rather smell a great meal simmering in the kitchen than overly pungent candles. However, we are partial to burning fig, pear, eucalyptus, or cedar scents. Joe loves gardenias and lilacs for their fragrance and peonies and dogwood for their sight. I love to look at more structural and organic floral forms and leave it up to him for scents and smells. Generally, we gravitate toward simple arrangements and only go big and bold when entertaining. Monochromatic is generally the rule with us (just no carnations, sunflowers, or red roses).

**A BEAUTIFUL BED** We sleep on Hillary Thomas custom sheeting for Harbinger. It's a great percale that's beautiful, too. A top and fitted sheet, a down duvet, and lots of pillows are a must. Typically four king-size pillows and one decorative pillow in front will suffice. A light blanket, a colorful coverlet at the foot of the bed, a soft rug under foot, blackout curtains, and earplugs for David are the little extras we need in the bedroom. On occasion, we will switch out our coverlet or duvet, but mostly it all remains the same.

**CREATURE COMFORTS** Fresh vegetables, hikes with our dog, sunny days, and warm ocean breezes contribute toward our sense of well-being. Quality time spent with friends and family, a good cocktail when needed, being surrounded by beautiful things, having a sense of purpose, and a dose of humor all add enjoyment to our life.

**MAKING AN ENTRANCE** Our entryway leads directly into the living room. Fortunately, it is an expansive space with a high-arched ceiling that fills with sunlight. Fresh flowers are plentiful, comfortable seating is abundant, and drinks are always at hand. Our dog, Fred, an Australian cattle and husky mix, serves as the welcoming committee. He always does a great job of making everyone feel like a guest of honor.

# MARY McDONALD
## ALWAYS INFUSE YOUR LIFE WITH PERSONALITY AND FLAIR.

Los Angeles–based interior designer Mary McDonald is a self-confessed serial homeowner and lover of all things glamorous. The Brentwood native and former milliner is equal parts glamour and gaiety. She currently owns two residences and has moved countless times during the last decade. Home is now a traditional three-story gated house, complete with brick paths, charming columned loggias, ornate pergolas, white railings, and balconies. Mary makes no secret that she prefers the faded elegance of days gone by and loves a touch of formality and luxe in every room.

When she set out to design her most recent dwelling, Mary's newly single status played a pivotal role in her creative directive. Craving a traditional atmosphere, she employed feminine florals, French chairs, delicate guéridons, and pretty stripes. "I am tired of everyone trying to be so hip. What happened to beautiful interiors?" Moving from a "much grander" residence offered a fresh start and demanded scrutinizing every square inch of space. Floors were painted white to radiate a light and happy feeling, while the front entrance was reconsidered. The current entry, a small vestibule that leads directly to the living area, was visually enlarged using a portion of the living room. Mary cleverly placed a large mahogany Regency pedestal table between the spaces to hold various bits and bobs from hors d'oeuvres to a bowl for keys. Depending on the designer's mood or latest find, objects constantly rotate on and off this multipurpose table.

No matter the home, Mary fashions seductive rooms infused with flair and old-school elegance. "I really am somewhat of a chameleon when it comes to design. I want to be a dozen different characters and I express myself as such through interiors." Lucite, chinoiserie, sterling silver, porcelain, and eighteenth-century French furniture always make a debut. Similarly, sentimentality guides many decisions. When faced with the choice to keep or discard a 1920s hand-painted bird-themed mural in a guest room, Mary crafted a canopy bed around the decor. She then added Lee Jofa chintz and devised custom slipper chairs swathed in a Cowtan & Tout mossy-green-and-ivory-striped fabric. "The mural had lasted so long it seemed a shame to get rid of it."

**DECORATIVE DETAILS** I cherish my small personal collections of various objects collected over time. Unusual patterns and vibrant color combinations also create an intriguing symphony of details and niceties. Stripes are wonderfully universal and can be modern or traditional. I don't believe that patterns necessarily have to match; however, the colors should work together and be of different scales. A geometric floor pattern (either painted, wood, or stone) adds visual interest, and I will always add a little chinoiserie to each of my rooms.

An avid collector of blue-and-white ceramics, the highly skilled hostess often brings together her passions outside. Massive groupings of large jardinières, overflowing with ferns and hydrangeas, fill the patio that doubles as an open-air dining room. "People always talk about bringing the outdoors in, but I would rather bring the indoors out." An all-weather, synthetic mock sea-grass rug sitting atop brick flooring, along with wrought-iron chairs, cobalt-blue garden stools, decorative pagodas, and wicker furniture further define the space. The cozy courtyard confirms her belief that living elegantly and being at ease are synonymous.

**MAKING AN ENTRANCE** Fresh flowers and a tray of cocktails are always well received by arriving guests, assuming, of course, it is after five o'clock. My own entryway is small but it functions beautifully. A pedestal table holds an assortment of decorative objects, and my style is to always add something current and a little zippy. I do love privacy; so just being able to close my door to the world makes me happy.

**FLOWERS AND FRAGRANCES** I love the scent of flowers first and foremost. Manuel Canovas candles come in a close second; their fragrance creates an opulent aromatic universe. I enjoy the Christmas holidays immensely and adore wintery pine scents that evoke the spirit of the season. Just a whiff of cedar or fir can bring back so many memories. In the right context, I appreciate all flowers, but I'm partial to striped roses. I particularly love 'Variegata di Bologna' and 'Honorine de Brabant'. The fact that nature is also a designer of kicky little stripes makes me smile.

**A BEAUTIFUL BED** I love a feather mattress cover, super-high-thread-count cotton sheets, shams (not pillowcases), and lightweight coverlets and a down comforter with a duvet at the end of the bed—I need one for tailoring and another for comfort. I am very partial to embroidered edges on my shams and the leading edge of my top sheet. E. Braun & Company's decorative embroideries, custom choices, and fabulous palette for bed linens are unsurpassed.

**CREATURE COMFORTS** Sometimes just having a pretty tablescape with fresh flowers adds to my aesthetic sense of well-being. Lots of sunlight makes me happy, too. Intangible comforts are harder to describe. A feeling that I am on the right path through my decisions and actions is important to me, as is a sense of humor about life and all of its foibles.

**ENTERTAINING THOUGHTS** Casual Sunday night dinners held on the early side, meals served outdoors, and Christmas parties are my favorite ways to entertain family and friends. When dining alfresco, low lighting and candles are a must—even in the summer. Don't forget outside lighting is just as important as indoor lighting, but no one wants tennis-court-style lighting blinding them at night. As for Christmas, anything goes; you can really get into an over-the-top spirit, decor-wise, with no need for excuses. The wrong illumination can ruin a party. Always use a ton of candles and 15-watt bulbs—it makes everything look magical.

# MIMI MADDOCK McMAKIN
## STYLISH LIVING IS WHATEVER MAKES YOU
## HAPPY AND WORKS IN YOUR LIFE.

Interior designer Mimi Maddock McMakin comes from a long line of notable relatives. A fourth-generation resident of Palm Beach, also known as the American Riviera, she lives a life as interesting as her family's history. Her grandfather, Sidney Maddock, built the 1902 Palm Beach Hotel, which burned down after catching fire from the same blaze that destroyed the Breakers in 1925. In 1891, her great-grandfather, Henry Maddock, built his family home, Duck's Nest, on the North End of the island. Named after the affectionate nickname, "Duckie," he called his wife, it is on record as the second-oldest residence in Palm Beach and is still owned by the Maddock family. The house was assembled in Brooklyn, New York, and floated down by barge on the Intracoastal Waterway to Palm Beach. "My dad always argued that it is actually the oldest house on the island," says Mimi.

The Duck's Nest property also houses the original Bethesda-by-the-Sea church, a Shingle-style deconsecrated structure that Mimi and her husband, Leigh, now call home. Large down-filled sofas take the place of pews, and a massive gaming table, which once belonged to the famous Bradley's Beach Club, is used for communing and dining. A giant butterfly kite hangs from the beamed and arched wooden ceiling and sails over a life-size cardboard cutout of Fabio thirty feet in the air. Two twelve-foot-diameter Balinese parasols are set open in the center of the room, reminding guests that the water is just steps away. Antique watercolors, photographs, fishing rods, bicycles, numerous carved wooden animals, and stuffed dolls share space on the walls, while an entire family of bears entertain on the roof of the exposed second level.

The floors are scuffed from a hundred years of traffic and little feet that learned to roller-skate and skateboard across the vast open spaces. It is difficult not to feel childlike in the playful home where everything is kept (and treasured), no matter how trivial. Over the years, friends have added to their quirky collection of scattered toys and memorabilia, making the old church their home, too. A serene portrait of Mimi's mother-in-law hangs where there was once an altar. "I know that she must

**DECORATIVE DETAILS** I can't live without flowers or greenery. I will go outside and cut anything pretty that catches my eye. Photographs are equally important. I can't imagine life without remembrances of my family constantly surrounding me. Memorable possessions (regardless of cost) and personal things that I value make me happy at home.

watch with amusement. We are an overwhelmingly sentimental family," admits Mimi.

During the spring and summer, Mimi spends much time in the garden surrounded by jasmine, gardenias, ylang-ylang, ginger, and angel's trumpets. The family refers to these flowering plants and trees as the "ladies." At night, the tropical air and ocean breezes are filled with their mixed perfumes; at times, it seems that each variety is competing to provide the greatest fragrance. In fact, Mimi would take her young, barefoot daughters outside at night to sniff deeply into the blooms. Each lady was a contestant and a winner would be declared. The angel's trumpet won most often. "There must have been something magical about being lifted up to nuzzle into their twelve-inch blooms." Her children now take their children outside at night, continuing the tradition of cheering on the ladies.

**MAKING AN ENTRANCE** Our home is not what one would describe as normal, yet it still lends itself to playfulness and warmth. I am always so excited when I walk through my door, and feel like a little child. Nothing is uncomfortable and I refuse to put something in my home because it is chic. I only live with things that I love. I am very sentimental and everything must have a story. The moment you enter this house you are transported to another world.

**FLOWERS AND FRAGRANCES** Our home usually smells like blooming jasmine and gardenias from the garden or my Metal perfume by Paco Rabanne. The scent was discontinued more than twenty years ago, but my children refuse to let me wear anything else. Whenever they find a bottle online or from an out-of-date foreign store, they buy a bottle. I probably have enough stockpiled to last for another twenty years.

**A BEAUTIFUL BED** A bedroom must have all of the little luxuries you love including the finest sheets you can afford. I keep an ottoman at the foot of the bed for our grandchildren and dogs to jump up on, and a cashmere throw to cuddle up in, even if it is warm outside. I adore beds that are so high off the ground that you have to climb onto them; and mattresses topped off with so much goose down that you practically fall in and someone has to come looking for you. Good lights for reading and fans are a must. This is one space where I don't care for extraneous objects.

**ENTERTAINING THOUGHTS** I like entertaining that is impromptu and as casual as possible. Playfulness and imagination is also important and I enjoy pulling out all of the stops when it comes to decor. Dinner outside under our bougainvillea tree is magical. Normally, I set the table both indoor and outdoors with my great-grandfather's china. Fun centerpieces made from found objects around the house are the best. Sometimes it is my husband's carved birds resting on large leaves, amusing toys, or small pictures of friends. It really doesn't matter what you put on the table, as long as it is pretty or witty.

# CHARLOTTE MOSS

## CONFIDENCE, CURIOSITY, DISCIPLINE, AND JOY
## IS THE WINNING FORMULA FOR STYLE.

"Most of my thoughts and desires revolve around houses," says Charlotte Moss, reflecting on her passions—writing, gardening, entertaining, reading, kayaking, collecting, and beachcombing. The designer-cum-businesswoman-cum-philanthropist is forever dreaming of more time spent at home and new creative endeavors. Each of her homes—whether it is her primary residence, a classic townhouse on New York's Upper East Side that she shares with her husband, Barry Friedberg, the couple's Shingle-style dwelling in East Hampton, or their seasonal retreat in Aspen—represents different aspects of her personality and pursuits. However, all echo Charlotte's preference for traditional elegance in a comfortable setting. They are all furnished with a profusion of French, Italian, and Swedish antiques. Charlotte particularly favors the straight lines of Louis XVI, Empire, and Directoire furniture. "Our homes speak to and are distillations of our lives, well lived and happy, of course."

While furniture may form the foundation of her rooms, it is Charlotte's meticulous eye for detail that most defines each space. As a collector of antique textiles, the designer is forever on the search for beautiful fabrics and is always up for a good hunt—a hobby that keeps each residence in a perpetual state of change. Reading and writing as well as journaling and creating elaborate scrapbooks of images that inspire her are also among her main passions. Each scrapbook compilation covers such themes as travel, family, gardening, entertaining, design, women of style, flower arrangements, and the "house in her head" (all are the subject of her latest book). A vast living room in her East Hampton country house that doubles as a library is testament to her obsession with books; twelve-foot-high bookcases

**MAKING AN ENTRANCE** Beautiful flowers, a potted jasmine, or a planter of fragrant herbs always reside in my hallway; it's a very welcoming way to greet guests and yourself every day. As the foyer is the last thing that I see before I take off for the day, and the first thing I witness when returning home, the memory that lingers must be a beautiful one laced with fragrance.

wrap two walls in the twenty-foot space. Just above a screened porch is Charlotte's private sanctum. A brightly lit space, designed originally as a sleeping porch, is now the nucleus for her collage and scrapbook work. Views of the garden and a canopied daybed provide the perfect escape to read and dream. "I am a big homebody," she admits.

When not working, writing, or traveling, Charlotte is just as likely to be found sitting in her book-lined Manhattan study, surrounded with photographs of her "favorite broads": Elsie de Wolfe, Coco Chanel, and Babe Paley. "We all need time alone to hear our own voice. Solitude is a good thing." Often it is simple mundane task, such as cleaning off a desk or organizing a closet, that offers a settling-down-take-care-of-business effect and one that makes space for more creative time. "Whenever I am home, I unconsciously drop my shoulders; I always feel safe, secure, vital, and alive."

**A BEAUTIFUL BED** A beautiful bed is the only bed to have, whatever your definition. Diana Vreeland said, "You have to have style; it helps you get up in the morning." I would add: what better way to do it than from a beautiful bed? When it comes to bedding, Jane Scott Hodges, the founder of Leontine Linens, does the greatest monograms. I also love the classic prints of D. Porthault on voile sheets, and Nancy Stanley Waud has created some very special embroidery for my bed. Longing for an opportunity to reimagine Pauline de Rothschild's bed at Château Mouton, as famously photographed by Horst for *Vogue*, I seized the moment when we bought our house in Aspen. My bed is tall and I have a perfect view of the mountains; it feels akin to floating on a cloud. I sometimes wonder, why ski?

**CREATURE COMFORTS** When I travel, I take along a down boudoir pillow and a light cashmere wrap that doubles as a throw. I like to have a piece of home on the road. For me, comfort is all about things that are familiar as well as great books, fresh flowers, and pleasing fragrances from flowers or the kitchen. An evening on the screened porch by the fire listening to the crickets and the ocean is my idea of a perfect night. Combine that with good friends, great wine, and what else do you need? *N'est ce pas?* In the end, if you are comfortable, others will be, too.

**FLOWERS AND FRAGRANCES** I adore all flowers, well, almost—gladiolas, birds of paradise, and calla lilies are just not on my radar. However, the most important thing about flowers is that you have them; it can be a single garden rose, a bunch of daisies, or wildflowers picked in a field. I prefer flowers that are informally arranged with a natural sense of ease and movement. Fragrance at all times is a bonus. Who can resist vines of jasmine and honeysuckle? I love mixing both in with my arrangements and adding tomato leaves, mint, and thyme. When it comes to centerpieces, moderation is best. You never want to overpower the food or overwhelm your guests.

**ENTERTAINING THOUGHTS** Ultimately, entertaining is about sharing and having fun. However, planning and organization are the keys to success. I know that making a checklist sounds elementary, but it is a must. You will be the most comfortable if you are relaxed, plus your guests will then be relaxed, too. It is also a time to be a little indulgent; a special takeaway for each guest or something to remember the party by is a wonderful gesture. It can be anything from a book to a CD or a few croissants for the morning after. Not necessary, just part of the fun.

**DECORATIVE DETAILS** Details are what distinguish our likes and passions. Whether it's a collection that speaks to personal interests and curiosity, found objects, the embellishments on upholstery, or the way things are arranged, these are the elements that make a room come to life. Details express who we are. I prefer rooms that showcase a creative and confident voice; ones that are decorated for the sake of decorating bore me to tears. Great decorating isn't about spending money; it's about seeing the beauty in simple things.

# AMANDA NISBET

## WHILE STYLE IS SUBJECTIVE, THOSE I CONSIDER STYLISH ALWAYS SEEM TO POSSESS AN INNATE, EFFORTLESS QUALITY.

Amanda Nisbet is as colorful and sophisticated as the Carnegie Hill apartment she calls home. The enchanting neighborhood, named for the mansion that Andrew Carnegie built at Fifth Avenue and 91st Street in 1901, rests on a hilly plateau that forms a small village on New York City's Upper East Side. From the moment you enter Amanda's world, you know that you are in for something delectable—a grown-up version of the corner candy store. Deep-orange drapery, pink china, lavender upholstered chairs, glossy celadon walls as smooth as glass, and laughter saturate the space. It's a home that not only looks good but also feels good. Each room of the prewar apartment seamlessly balances function and style with classicism and modernism in surprising and interesting ways. A rock-crystal lamp contentedly lives with a contemporary photograph by Alex Prager and a painted table from designer Nancy Lancaster's own house. But don't let the carefully curated collection mislead you; this is first and foremost a home for family, friends, and entertaining. "My home is the culmination of everything that I love. It is my favorite place to vacation," she remarks, and then adds, "It's my escape from the world. I love nothing more than being at home and sitting with my family in front of a roaring, crackling fire."

Although Amanda is attracted to the styles of Billy Baldwin and David Hicks, her grandmother was her most significant design influence—she inspired the one-time actress to leave the stage and consider a career in decorating. An "unpaid decorator" is how Amanda describes her grandmother, whose portrait hangs against the

**ENTERTAINING THOUGHTS** I am not a precise, measured cook. Thus, baking is too tedious for me. I do love fresh pasta tossed with a bunch of herbs and a crumbly Parmigiano Reggiano. I am partial to a bold red wine, perfect for a languorous yet lively evening. Autumn is my favorite season for gathering those I love. Everyone has returned home from summer vacation and back to their daily routine. Entertaining is a great way to mix up the scheduled day to day. It's also the perfect season to cuddle up with warm drinks and catch up with family and friends. All you need is food, plenty of wine on hand, and great music. Everything else will fall into place.

**CREATURE COMFORTS**
I'm a Taurus and I love all things beautiful—clothes, jewelry, shoes, bags, food, and decor. I am equally fond of art, books, luxurious linens, spinning classes, yoga, my family, laughter, and love. All of these things contribute toward my sense of emotional well-being. I don't much care for formulaic, impersonal rooms nor do I like pretense.

brown Venetian plaster walls of the dining room opposite a large painting by artist James Nares. "Some of the nicest things in this room belonged to my grandmother. She was very glamorous, but along with all the glamour, I wanted my dining room to be cozy and modern. I added brown to temper the space and shades of lavender and soft blues to lighten the mood."

While aesthetics are important, comfort at home is paramount. One is never sacrificed for the other. "I see the scrapes and scuffs born by a home as analogous to the fine laughter lines of a well-lived life." Never one to follow a strict formula or set of rules, Amanda does, however, live by the idea that every room in the apartment must mix the playful with the serious, and luxury with affordability. "Everything doesn't have to be wildly expensive when you decorate. I like to think I walk a very careful line between tasteful and tacky."

**MAKING AN ENTRANCE** An entrance hall is the perfect place to pique curiosity. I like for people to wonder what lies around the next corner. In my own hallway, art, lighting, and texture are important. When I come home at the end of the day, I always feel serene and uplifted. I hope that everyone who enters our home experiences a genuine sense of love and beauty. But most of all, it is important that I have created a welcoming environment.

**DECORATIVE DETAILS** The most important details are objects that provide a connection to family, friends, and creative people. These details are essential to my daily life. Family photographs, my children's artwork, and art by favorite artists make me happy. I adore unexpected pairings, fun uses of color, good food, and great music. My tastes in music are as varied as my tastes in design. I like to listen to everything from Kiri Te Kanawa to Beyoncé to Wiz Khalifa to Wilco. I think Dorothy Draper had it right when she said that it is just as disastrous to have the wrong accessories in your room as it is to wear sport shoes with an evening dress.

**FLOWERS AND FRAGRANCES** My favorite scents are lilies, mimosa, jasmine, peonies, and gardenia. When it comes to flowers I adore ranunculus for their vibrancy, depth of color, and wonderful sculptural quality. Each stem meanders and follows its own path within the bouquet. They always make me smile. Peonies are another perfect flower for both sight and scent. Their dense labyrinth of layer-upon-layer fullness is divine. I tend to gravitate toward jewel-toned flowers in shades of deep boysenberry, chartreuse, olive green, and warm orange.

**A BEAUTIFUL BED** My bed is one of my favorite respites from a chaotic day. I love gorgeous linens and have a slew of custom designs that I utilize for my varying moods. Typically, I use sateen sheets, a duvet, a cashmere blanket, six down sleeping pillows, three king shams, and one bolster pillow. For ambiance, I add a yummy Diptyque candle and fresh peonies or lilacs. A fabulous room needs not only a beautiful bed but also good lighting and someone you love to join you at night.

# MICHELLE NUSSBAUMER

## STYLISH LIVING IS COMPLETE, UNADULTERATED COMFORT WITHOUT FORSAKING BEAUTY.

The unassuming facade of Michelle and Bernard Nussbaumer's 1940s Regency-style dwelling provides little hint to the magnificence that lurks behind its walls and neat rows of azalea bushes. Set back from the narrow, curving roads in one of Dallas's preeminent neighborhoods, it is a beautifully aged brick structure. Entering the vast double front door is akin to being handed first-class tickets to a visual voyage around the world. Asian and Middle Eastern decorative details, united with rich fabrics from India and European antiques, set against whimsical wall treatments, are symbolic of her urbane style. What might look like seemingly disparate influences to the untrained eye is precisely what inspires Michelle and comes alive under her spell.

The native Texan developed her flair for drama while attending Southern Methodist University, where she pursued a degree in theater. Though originally drawn to the stage and acting, she found her calling during a set design course. The opportunity to design her own space soon followed with her marriage to her Swiss film producer husband. The couple moved to Rome for a brief period, where they started a family and Michelle began a love affair with antiques. Looking to immerse herself in the culture and furnish their villa on Via Appia Antica, she became fluent in the language and familiar with the area's many locales. Frequent houseguests soon fell for the emerging designer's stylish abode, and at their request, Michelle joined them on shopping sprees throughout Italy.

**MAKING AN ENTRANCE** The entrance is your opening act. Don't hold back. My husband and I like for people to be enchanted, feel welcomed, and wonder what is beyond the front door. To create drama, I use large-scale items and modern art. Likewise, wallpaper on the ceiling or a wall, a dramatic paint color, or a patterned floor always creates a "wow" factor. I want our guests to be smitten by the surroundings and long to return.

After returning to Dallas, she opened Ceylon et Cie, her 10,000-square-foot antiques emporium, and continued filling her own home with a growing collection of treasures while decorating for clients around the world. Everything in the Nussbaumer residence reflects her global influences and love of family and travel (time is split between Dallas, Switzerland, and Mexico). Though fearless when it comes to style and design, always combining the precious and the playful, Michelle notes that suitable furnishings and proportions are of utmost importance. "Our house is a place where the kids, dogs, and friends can relax and unwind." The family of six (and their many dogs) live in every inch of the home. Priceless sofas and chairs that have traveled back and forth across the ocean are protected from wear and tear under decorative slipcovers that have been washed countless times. "Form nor style should never suffer due to function. My family's comfort always comes first."

**CREATURE COMFORTS** I love a well-designed room full of laughter, my favorite people, and lots of craziness. There is nothing I adore more than a hot bubble bath, having all of my children at home, and our slobbery Great Dane, Loretta. Having raised four children in this house, it really is our family home.

**DECORATIVE DETAILS** Few things are more important than multiple sources of light. I love using lighting to create a feeling of intimacy and to define areas of a room. Often I use lamps that cast an interesting pattern or one great chandelier. I also avoid bright illumination by using dimmers and low-wattage light bulbs. Other essential decorative details include vibrant colors, personal collections, great architecture, and antique carpets.

**FLOWERS AND FRAGRANCES** Rive Gauche Yves Saint Laurent perfume, handmade incense from India, and Ceylon gardenia candles permeate our house. Peonies are amazing for their beauty and gardenias for their intoxicating scent. I love to mix in fresh bouquets with mint from my herbal garden. When it comes to flowers, I normally opt for red, red, and more red inside my home and only white in my garden. I will, however, cut and bring in whatever is blooming in my garden, even herbs or vegetables.

**A BEAUTIFUL BED** The bedroom is your personal refuge and most private space of all. I like to use luxurious textures, soft textiles, and calming colors. Typically, I prefer a single color with varying hues rather than mixing different ones together. Pressed Italian linens, down pillows, and a feather topper are my bedding wardrobe staples. We don't change linens with the seasons, but rather with our mood, which is often. It may be cashmere one day and velvet the next.

**ENTERTAINING THOUGHTS** We love to entertain year-round. Any time that I can pull it together, people seem to show up. A mixed crowd and an unexpected menu are always satisfying. For impromptu dinners, we usually serve grilled fish and vegetables; in cooler months a lamb tagine or a beef vindaloo is perfect. There is always extra wine and batches of pastry puffs in the freezer just waiting for friends to stop by for a visit.

# DAVID OLIVER

STYLISH LIVING IS BREATHING IN AND ABSORBING
THE QUALITIES OF A PLACE . . . THEN BREATHING OUT AGAIN.

Open the glossy, black front door of the London townhouse David Oliver shares with his partner, Veere Grenney, and you are lured into a very colorful world. Chablis-green silk velvet walls, chintz smoking chairs, an aquamarine sofa, Cognac-colored Fortuny damask, mustard cashmere walls, and gold satin binding all live together in sophisticated harmony. Christened the "rock star" of color by the press, David, design director of London's Paint & Paper Library, is a man who understands the power of color. Whether in the form of pictures, wall paint, carpets, wallpaper, furniture, or fabric, it plays a pivotal role in his surroundings. It only takes a few moments with the charming Australian to appreciate that a highly attuned aesthetic underpins his style and his personality. Not just at home, but in all areas of life. "Everyday color allows us a brilliant opportunity to make a statement. Whether decorating a house or getting dressed, I see both as an occasion to make not just a statement, but a stylish one."

David's infectious personality and addiction to color is eclipsed only by his passion for photography and travel with family and friends. Mixing with locals in another country, witnessing firsthand their everyday life, and capturing it all on film is one of his chief obsessions. Such an experience always bestows him with fresh ideas to take home and incorporate into his own world. An explorer by nature and artist by training, David traveled a long and colorful trail before founding his paint and wallpaper company. He moved to Madrid in the early 1990s to see firsthand the great paintings of Goya, Velázquez, El Greco, and Picasso. Not knowing a soul or speaking the language, he stayed for one year painting, and then exhibited in a one-man show at Galeria Mar Estrada. The next year he moved to the Republic of Ireland and lived in an eighteenth-century

**DECORATIVE DETAILS** Details not only help to define a home but they also add true personal expression. I like to think of them as the punctuation marks in a sentence. I love the Victorian tradition of curiosities and have many scattered on my desk and bookcases in the library. Each provokes a sense wonder. Even if they are strange, humble keepsakes, they remind me of excursions abroad and special occasions with friends. In my dressing room, I adore small personal possessions, such as silver-framed photographs of friends and family. It's my private space to reflect on the day's events and just think.

**FLOWERS AND FRAGRANCES** I prefer to rotate plants according to the season—orange blossom in the summer, jasmine in the fall, lime in the spring, and silver wattle or mimosa in the winter. Each fills the air with distinct seasonal notes and allows me to enjoy and appreciate each season. At Christmastime, I adore terra-cotta pots of paper whites with their strongly fragrant flowers. Whenever possible, I like to have a cutting garden with roses and dahlias for small vases that I place by the bed or on the table for lunch. I don't much care for tortured flower arrangements. Give me cut flowers that look as if they've just come from the garden.

Georgian house with the County Louth Master of Fox Hounds and his family. During that time, he used their ballroom and conservatory as a studio. David happily takes the road less traveled looking for out-of-the-way gems, and finds staying at five-star resorts "pure hell."

Always craving adventure, he is not one for settling on one home or locale. While daily life takes place in London, he and Veere regularly escape to their Suffolk cottage, built as a Palladian fishing temple and folly, or their 1950s French Colonial–style home in Tangier. "I will always opt for homes that are open to the influence of the surroundings and draw on its context and contents for inspiration." He believes that living a full life means creating a space that is colorful, welcoming, collected, and comfortable. It is a philosophy that permeates his life each day and comes as naturally as breathing.

**MAKING AN ENTRANCE** A doorway or entry hall is a great place to make a strong first impression and call attention to the most attractive features of the space. In London, I like my front door to be black and very, very glossy. I think it looks so incredibly smart and gives the feeling of depth and perspective. Black is also a color associated with elegance. The entry is an area where I can be experimental, have fun, create maximum impact, and, above all, welcome my guests.

**A BEAUTIFUL BEDROOM** Ideally, I prefer to sleep in a four-poster or tester canopy bed. I love the sense of privacy and security, and I always want my feet facing south so that I can get the maximum amount of sun. My bed linens are always starched white Irish linen. Sometimes I opt for embroidery, but oddly enough, never in another color. Additionally, I need good lighting, an armchair, books, fabric-lined walls, blackout curtains, and a water jug. Music is a must. I have 250 songs on my iPod that were all selected by friends; it's a wonderful, eclectic collection.

**CREATURE COMFORTS** In the spring, I love listening to the morning birds sing outside my bedroom. And, in the winter, I wait for the first peaceful snowfall, when everything seems to stop and go quiet. Whenever it's warm outside, I enjoy nothing more than pottering about in the greenhouse or lying in the sun with piles of books on the weekends. The only thing to top a perfect sunny afternoon at home is a midday swim and a hazy heat to crack the water on my back.

**ENTERTAINING THOUGHTS** Dining alfresco is my favorite way to entertain, and in the summer it's all about barbecue. Perhaps it's being Australian or growing up on a cattle farm, either way I love to barbecue fresh, organic meat. And few things in life are better than picnics on the grass in the middle of a field. Whether it's eating under a fig tree in Tangier or an apple tree in England, I find sitting outside with friends to be such a treat. It's an easy way to entertain with flair, and it provides a certain colonial charm. My favorite picnic tip—don't forget to bring salt. Your guests will be pleasantly surprised and grateful. As for drinks, you can't go wrong with Laurant-Perrier Champagne, a New Zealand Sauvignon Blanc, a Spanish Rioja, or an Argentinean Malbec.

# ALEX PAPACHRISTIDIS

## STYLE IS LIVING LIFE TO THE FULLEST AND
## NEVER COMPROMISING ON BEAUTY.

If pressed to describe the Upper East Side apartment of interior designer Alex Papachristidis and his partner, Scott Nelson, "resplendent" would be at the top of the adjective list. A beautiful explosion of rich colors, luxurious textures, and elaborate patterns create a formidable backdrop to their glamorous life. Well-read books spill from the bookshelves, while evocative art and antiques fill every corner. Each room is a mix of periods, but the eighteenth century is a particular favorite, further adding to the layers of interesting objects and elements. "Even the best examples of modern furniture reference eighteenth-century shapes and silhouettes," says Alex.

Your senses are heightened the moment you enter this sumptuous abode. A back-to-back gilt black lacquer chinoiserie bookcase floats in the center of a tented hallway that is covered in an exuberant Oscar de la Renta striped fabric, and a rare portrait of the Duke and Duchess of Windsor smiles at each passerby. The designer's eye for luxury and lush walls are evident throughout the apartment, especially the living room. A custom chinoiserie wallpaper, inspired by Jayne Wrightsman's Palm Beach living room, provides an exotic backdrop for a pair of gilded bronze guéridons (a gift from Alex's mother), a Jensen side table, a gilded tree-branch coffee table, a black and gold commode, a Louis Philippe rope stool, and a Prussian blue Christopher Spitzmiller lamp designed by Alex. Rich fabrics in shades of royal blue and plum govern the space. The room is a mix of lacquer, natural wood, gilded bronze, and painted and gilded wood finishes, creating an elegant, collected atmosphere. For the mix master, balance and layering of materials and textures is crucial.

Syrie Maugham, Billy Baldwin, Elsie de Wolfe, John Fowler, Pauline de Rothschild, Mona Bismarck, and Sister Parish are the style icons that have influenced the designer's aesthetic. However, it is his mother whom Alex credits as the source for his deep appreciation of all things beautiful. As a young boy, he soaked

**CREATURE COMFORTS** It is important that everything looks beautiful, but I honestly believe cleanliness is next to godliness. I am very visual and beauty calms my soul and keeps me in high spirits. A happy home is one that is well stocked and properly maintained with every convenience needed to make life a little easier each day. I enjoy spending time surrounded by things that inspire and bring comfort and joy.

## MAKING AN ENTRANCE

Our tented entrance hall is both playful and grand, much like the entire apartment. Once inside, you are transported into a fantasy world, touched by whimsical style and romantic luxury. Warmth, elegance, and an inviting atmosphere are all distinguishing features that I have created in my home; the hallway decor lays the groundwork.

up the glitz and glamour of his parents' international lifestyle; traveling, visiting museums, and going to the theater, the opera, and films stimulated his creative development. "We traveled constantly and moved all around the Upper East Side. Once my mother took us to Greece for the summer, and we stayed for two years. My mother was truly an Auntie Mame figure."

Possessing an experienced eye, Alex is a taskmaster when it comes to details. He staunchly maintains that every home should have depth of character and be filled with conversation pieces. Not simply interesting objects, but things that possess style and tell a story. His approach is very old-school, and he likes his home to have a collected and layered feel. "I must sit in a chair or touch a piece of fabric before making a judgment." He prefers to keep matched sets of anything (except for bedside lamps and dining room chairs) to a minimum. "A room should not look like a pair party." At the core of his philosophy, Alex believes that great interiors should be beautiful and usable, not something viewed in passing.

**DECORATIVE DETAILS** I am not big on rules, but I am a stickler for details. I am crazy about exotic patterns, prints, and lush wall upholstery. I take great pleasure in mixing each element in an interesting way. Getting the balance right in any room requires careful layering of materials and textures. My collection of books, furniture, and artwork have been meticulously chosen to create the right atmosphere and mix. Beyond the decorative details, few things bring greater joy to our home than entertaining our friends, family, and spending time with our beloved Yorkshire terrier, Teddy.

**FLOWERS AND FRAGRANCES** I prefer the flowery scents of gardenia, tuberose, and white flowers in their pure form. As for candles, Blue Garden Classic by Nest is a wonderful mix of blue hydrangea, hyacinth, and forget-me-nots. I love the fresh green notes. Peonies and garden roses in bright, rich, strong colors are unparalleled for both scent and sight.

**A BEAUTIFUL BED** I consider the master bedroom an important living space, and the bed is always the focal point. I want a bed that is both lush and comfortable. I use six down pillows, a crisp white fitted sheet, a white duvet with custom-colored embroidery, an Indian quilt or custom-made quilt at the foot of the bed, and a down mattress pad for extra warmth in the winter. I never use a top sheet; I don't like to feel as if I am getting tangled while sleeping.

**ENTERTAINING THOUGHTS** I adore a buffet dinner. You never have to worry if someone cancels or brings last-minute guests; it's a very relaxed way to entertain. I always make a point of having vegetarian options. Not only are more people vegetarians these days, but it also shows care and consideration. Gifts for your host is always a thoughtful gesture, but I never send flowers before a party, always the day after so that no one feels obligated to use the flowers in their decorating scheme. I prefer to bring a book or a wonderful box of Teuscher chocolates.

# ROBERT PASSAL
## I BELIEVE IN LIVING EVERY DAY TO ITS FULLEST POTENTIAL.

Despite thirty-year-old avocado-green shag carpeting and crumbling plaster, interior designer Robert Passal knew his once-dilapidated Manhattan apartment had great potential. While many would turn for the door on first viewing, Robert fell in love. Recognizing that the 1927 structure had great bones and much potential, he purchased the property on a whim. Even though the home possessed fantastic architectural structure, all of the original, charming details were long gone. To restore interior appeal, Robert designed coffered ceilings, ornate crown molding, and custom cabinetry that replicated the prewar craftsmanship and also created a foundation for his extensive collection of art, furniture, and accessories.

A narrow vestibule leading from the elevator now opens to a saffron-yellow art-filled hallway packed with unexpected drama. A gold-leaf wall sculpture by Brett Murray from the series *Golden Truths* reads, "What Would Oprah Say?" and a smiling Jackie Kennedy by artist Alex Cao looms large over a marble table supported by two blackamoor figures. Soft lighting from table lamps cast a glow over the inviting space, further adding to the allure.

The living room is a study in sexy, layered luxe and the high-gloss white lacquered walls give the designer unlimited freedom in changing his furniture and color palette. A strong, graphic Stark rug anchors the room and supports a velvet sofa, a Victorian horn table, and a nineteenth-century periwinkle bergère chair that once belonged to the late decorator David Barrett. A pair of Michael Lucero Foo dogs swathed in colorful discarded Missoni wool stand guard on either side of the fireplace mantel, and a mirrored ceiling fixture from the old Rainbow Room accentuates the spellbinding space.

In the adjoining dining-room-cum-guest-room-cum-study, Robert designed a foldaway table and a long chocolate-colored banquette that also houses a bed, creating a flexible space for entertaining and guests. The often-used table is adorned with mismatched seating that includes metal Jensen chairs and Russian Regency chairs covered in rich leopard-print fabric. A collection of salon-style framed nudes

**DECORATIVE DETAILS** Without a doubt, fresh flowers bring a room to life and allow me to vary the accent colors in my space. However, carefully chosen art and accessories give a space soul. No matter how wonderful the furnishings, they don't sing until they are accessorized. A room that is richly layered in memories and individualized collections is what makes a house a home.

(many found on eBay) and a pair of Claude and Francois-Xavier's wool Lalanne sheep watch over the room. "My look is a mix of high, low, modern, and traditional. I buy things that invoke thought or make me smile. Sometimes both."

Robert's juxtaposition of periods and styles carry over to his cocoonlike bedroom. Plush cotton velvet fabric, in a shade of deep vermilion, upholsters the walls and muffles the sounds of New York traffic. Zebra carpeting further softens the space, while a 1920s plaster ceiling mounted fixture by Serge Roche seductively reflects light. Lying in bed reading, chatting on the phone, or checking email are favorite luxuries. "When I was younger, I associated being in bed with laziness. Now, I view my bed as a true place of solace."

**MAKING AN ENTRANCE** A great entryway should be engrossing, tell a story, and welcome guests. I want friends to be comfortable in my home and feel as if they can remove their shoes, sit anywhere they choose, or curl up on the sofa. In my own hallway, I strive to create anticipation and fashion a space that alludes to what will unfold around each corner. Fresh flowers, great art, proper lighting with dimmers, and burning candles all add to the allure.

**FLOWERS AND FRAGRANCES** I adore the smell of a wood fire and I am lucky to have a working fireplace. During the months that I can't burn logs, I light a Diptyque Feu de Bois candle. The woody essence is such a sophisticated scent. Throughout the holidays, nothing is better than steeping cinnamon, nutmeg, and cloves on the stove. Like Jackie Kennedy, I can't get enough of hot-pink peonies, especially in a stark white vessel.

**CREATURE COMFORTS** Nothing beats long walks, driving alone, sharing a meal with friends, journaling, exercise, reading, spending time in bed, finding time to write, being surrounded by art, and silence.

**A BEAUTIFUL BED** A great bed needs a great foundation; a handmade Savoir mattress is the very best. I prefer an all-white bed in the warmer seasons, often with contrasting embroidered detailing, and a knit cotton blanket in warm contrasting tones. In the winter, I switch to chocolate browns and navy blue with a goose-down duvet. For me, Sferra percale sheeting is a must; I think sateen can be a bit too fussy. My one "never" is a set of matching bedding; you can't achieve a lush look without multiple layers and a variety of textures.

**ENTERTAINING THOUGHTS** I always keep my social gatherings simple so that I can spend time with my guests. My recipe for easy entertaining is an uncomplicated cocktail, takeout served on fine china, and a bottle of fantastic wine. A well-stocked pantry is a must, and I have learned to quickly prepare a fabulous cheese platter. My favorite staples include Marcona almonds, Pepperidge Farm goldfish, dried Turkish figs, fresh berries, cured meats, and Sicilian olives. For overnight guests, I like to have all the makings of a continental breakfast. If you keep a great loaf of bread and good coffee in the freezer, everyone wins.

# KATHARINE POOLEY

## MY STYLE IS QUINTESSENTIALLY BRITISH: UNDERSTATED LUXURY WITHOUT SACRIFICING COMFORT OR COHERENCE.

An innate sense of adventure, a love of history, and multicultural influences form the foundation of Katharine Pooley's design aesthetics and philosophy. The London-based interior designer has visited more than 250 countries, driven a team of sled dogs to the North Pole, crossed the Sahara on horseback, and restored a 450-year-old Scottish castle. The castle that she shares with her family and siblings was originally built in 1560 by the Ogilvys of Airlie. Eighty years after construction, Forter Castle, as it is now known, was destroyed by the Campbells of Argyll as a result of feuding between the clans. The castle lay in ruins for more than three hundred years before Robert Pooley and his daughter Katharine resurrected the pile of rubble. "My father had driven past the crumbling castle for thirty years, always dreaming of restoring a small piece of Scottish history," she recalls.

From the beginning, the father-daughter duo worked closely with Scottish Heritage. An oak tree growing in the center of the derelict house first had to be removed, and the missing roof restored. During the early stages of restoration, the underlying flagstone floor was discovered amid the wreckage, offering clues to the original structure. After two years of meticulous renovations, Katharine took over the interiors, carefully restoring each room. "It was important for me to understand and marry cultural influences and local history." Swords, their coat of arms, wool rugs, and the family tartan now grace the thick stone-walled rooms. The Great Hall, spanning the width of the first floor, boasts a vast stone fireplace, mahogany bookcases, and a dining table that seats sixteen. Oil paintings, oversized tapestries, and intricate murals evoke the past and trace the castle's visual history. An elaborate painted ceiling mural depicts the traditional Scottish song "The Bonnie House of Airlie." Katharine commissioned artist Jenny Merredew to create the mural in the tradition of many local historic buildings. The ballad recalls the destruction of Forter Castle. For amusement, Katharine's brother, Sebastian, often sings the ballad at family gatherings.

**DECORATIVE DETAILS** Family heirlooms not only tell a great story but also bring a home to life. I particularly adore the exquisite hand-painted ceiling in the Great Hall depicting the castle's fascinating history. Personal relics are fundamental, as are photographs, books, and artwork. Most everything around me has been collected over time. For beauty and comfort, I will never forgo cashmere throws.

A narrow spiral staircase leads to five bedrooms named after Katharine's siblings and the spectacular Laird's Room with dramatic views of the Highlands—a retreat unto itself. Originally two rooms, it is now one large space with the same dimensions as the Great Hall, dominated by a four-poster bed and a freestanding rolltop bath hidden behind folding screens. The castle's tight twisting staircase, while charming, proved less than ideal when relocating furnishings. A few things "got stuck," prompting a call to a nearby antiques dealer. Some pieces had to be cut in half and clamped together again. "One thing I have learned," says Katharine, "if you have the will you will find a way to make things work."

When not dividing time between London and Oxfordshire, Katharine and her family are quick to return to Scotland. Time away includes no Internet access, as well as cooking, playing games, reading, walking, and enjoying the simple things in life. It's a dwelling where she feels instantly happy and relaxed.

**MAKING AN ENTRANCE** A welcoming focal point that draws people into a home is something we all desire, but I also think that a magnificent front door is hugely important. An entrance offers visitors a first impression of your home. I love a door with strong character that comes as a result of great craftsmanship. When you enter Forter, warm colors and wool tartan rugs create a cozy ambiance, an especially important quality in cold climates.

**FLOWERS AND FRAGRANCES** Nothing can replace the refreshing vibrancy of flowers. I gravitate toward classic white flowers with a fresh, sophisticated feel. White peonies are a favorite. I also fill my home with the smell and warmth of candles. When I created Katharine Pooley candles for my boutique in London, we infused each with some of my most treasured scents—jasmine, water lilies, and green orchid.

**A BEAUTIFUL BED** The bedroom must be a comfortable, calm, and welcoming retreat at the end of the day. The ultimate bedroom accessory is wonderful linens with beautiful detailing. Bespoke details give the bed a truly unique look and are worth the investment—not to mention that quality linen ages beautifully and can be handed down through generations. Crisp white linen, layered with wonderfully textured pillows and a beautiful plush blanket, is perfect for chilly nights.

**ENTERTAINING THOUGHTS** I am a big fan of entertaining at home and I love classic aperitifs and nibbles. Nothing compares to relaxing with loved ones of all ages, eating delicious food, and drinking wonderful wines. Soft lighting, great music, and glowing candles always make guests feel relaxed and at ease. My idea of true luxury is hiring a chef to come to my home and cook up a fantastic feast for very special occasions.

# SUZANNE RHEINSTEIN

## LIVING WELL EVERY DAY IS MORE IMPORTANT THAN GETTING YOUR HOUSE TOGETHER FOR A SPECIAL OCCASION.

"I have always cared deeply about tradition and architecture," says Suzanne Rheinstein, interior designer and owner of Los Angeles's Hollyhock. Even as a child, Suzanne was enchanted by the cultural history of her native New Orleans and captivated by the Creole cottages, shotgun houses, gardens, neoclassical buildings, and dilapidated churches. Pressing against the glass of antiques shops in the French Quarter, and staring at pretty objects is a favorite childhood memory. Her love of interior and garden design (she is passionately devoted to both) was fostered through family outings and books. "I can always describe what a house looks like in any novel. From Proust's salons to the wonderful architecture in *Anna Karenina*—I love it all."

For more than thirty years, Suzanne and her husband, Fred, have lived in a 1914 Georgian Revival–style house in the Hancock Park neighborhood of Los Angeles. Shutters close with winches, fireplaces draw beautifully, the woodwork is simple but finely detailed, French doors open onto green gardens, and rooms are perfectly proportioned. A 1920s Chickering piano belonging to Fred's family dominates the light-filled entrance hall. When the Rheinsteins entertain, which is often, guests are greeted to the tinkling sound of jazz. Off the vast hall, a varied collection of French chairs and a Regency sofa set atop a straw rug encircle the inviting, sunny living room. However, it's the library, added in the 1930s, that beckons friends to gather, sit, visit, play cards, and relax. The library is also the room where dinner is served on trays in front of a fire during cooler months.

Suzanne has earned a reputation for mixing neoclassical genres in a graceful and unfussy way. She is also the first to admit that her look has evolved over the years, but its core components have not changed. "I've never been one to move from style to style," she says. The one constant has always been her love of everything neoclassical, no matter the country of origin. Proportions and the layout of a room

**CREATURE COMFORTS** So many little things make me smile: ironed sheets, cloth napkins, iced-coffee made with my Toddy coffee maker, fresh lemon verbena for tisane, herbs outside the kitchen door, my husband's delicious roast chicken on Sunday nights, small batches of bourbon with Meyer lemons from our tree, listening to Yo-Yo Ma, waxed wooden floors, and masses of beeswax candles burning around the house.

**DECORATIVE DETAILS** Books, lamps, candles, old candlesticks, and orchids—not the white phalaenopsis variety but the odd chartreuse ones or green lady's slippers—in weathered clay pots fill our home. A big oval painted basket on a chest in the upstairs hall is always filled with masses of green foliage and pepper berries. It's delightful to see on our way to bed each night.

are equally important, and she likes objects that are not too serious. Antiques, especially quirky one-of-a-kind pieces, and the slightly off-kilter Italian Directoire style spark her design imagination. "I feel that imperfection—that is to say, things that are not too grand or a little wonky—lends comfort to a room."

Other qualities the passionate gardener holds in high regard are solid structure and good bones, both indoors and in the garden. "English decorator Nancy Lancaster said it best: 'You must first have a plan and good bones.' Once you have that in place you have great leeway in adding the things that you love. It's the same for gardens as it is for interior design." Her own garden is proof. A marriage of loose and formal plants live in harmony with an herb garden, textured boxwoods, and a silver carpet of lamb's ear. Flowers and foliage from the garden infuse the Rheinstein's home, and fresh herbs are always in the kitchen. Their house is a perfect example of indoor-outdoor living at its best.

**MAKING AN ENTRANCE** Our entrance hall is commodious without being grand. The café au lait patterned linen diaper walls help to soften the space, while the red grosgrain trim adds a lighthearted touch. Old Oriental rugs blanket the floor and several lamps cast pools of warm light, making the space very cozy. If there is a party, someone is always playing piano and everyone gathers around. A few antique blue-and-white vases, filled with flowers, live atop the piano—party or no party.

**FLOWERS AND FRAGRANCES** I like delicious smells, but not obvious ones. Wood fires on cool evenings, the scent of figs in the summer, and spicier tones in the winter. Pots of citrus (lemons, limes, kumquats) scattered around the pool have a wonderful aroma that drifts through the windows and into the house. Many of our fragrant outdoor flowers (stephanotis, old roses, white heliotrope) can be brought inside. And unless it's Christmas or some supergala occasion, I prefer flowers that look as if they have come straight from the garden.

**A BEAUTIFUL BED** Few things are lovelier than crisply pressed cotton sheets in white or ecru with beautiful monograms or simple embroidery around the edges. For decorative details, I adore thin silk quilts from Vietnam and India in solid colors as a light duvet or bedcover. In colder months, a fur throw is a wonderful luxury. Euro square pillows are great for reading in bed, as is a good reading lamp. As a general rule, I avoid masses of coordinated decorative pillows and duvet covers.

**ENTERTAINING THOUGHTS** I use plates that came from my mother, grandmother, and my husband's family. I have hundreds of forks that I have collected over the years, and I always buy huge damask napkins when I am in France, usually with someone else's monogram—they cover your entire lap and then some. We always enjoy having our neighbors over for a drink and a game of dominoes. Most recently, we have been playing International Rummy, a very addictive game taught to us by our friends William Yeoward and Colin Orchard.

## KATIE RIDDER AND PETER PENNOYER
### STYLISH LIVING IS MATERIAL COMFORT EXPRESSED THROUGH FURNITURE AND COLLECTIONS ACCUMULATED OVER TIME.

Architect Peter Pennoyer and his wife, interior designer Katie Ridder, know how to blend life, work, and play. Their 1920s residence in a tiny village in Westchester, New York, is a storybook example of the couple's combined talents and collaboration. The Queen Anne–style structure they share with their three children and dachshund brims with color, pattern, and flights of the imagination. Charles Lewis Bowman, a former McKim, Mead & White draftsman and master of English-style architecture, designed the multistory family home. Bowman populated the town with several charming Cotswold-esque cottages during the early part of the twentieth century. From the road, their house appears diminutive, with one large gable and a whimsical portico. The interiors however are expansive.

Just inside the front door a marble table designed by the duo anchors the entrance and a tall clock sits atop the original black-and-white flooring. A series of five floors and half floors ascend from the open foyer. The unusual design and many levels wind up and around the vast hall. The stairs create an elaborate path from the first to the second floors, which accentuates the feeling of light and space. Each corner of the home has a distinct personality, and proportions vary greatly from room to room. "Mr. Bowman created an incredible sense of scale. Our house is full of clever architectural tricks," says Peter. To add their own playful touch, the couple hired a decorative artist to coat the twisting balustrade with a glossy ruby-red paint and silver-leaf trim.

Over the years, the house had undergone various renovations, some more successful than others. Together Katie

**MAKING AN ENTRANCE** Entryways don't need a lot of furniture, but they do need to be well furnished and designed. We never want our front hall to look decorated, but rather we prefer that it delight all who enter. Every entry benefits from a table for mail and miscellany, interior and exterior doormats, and an interesting chandelier, as well as a combination of lighting (both overhead and eye level).

and Peter removed overly ornate details, refinished mahogany paneling in the library, and painted over wood floors in the dining room and cabinetry in the kitchen. "Our style is the not-always-easy balance between harmony and novel interpretation," says Peter. "It is somewhere between the comfort of idealized perfection and the challenges of reality," adds Katie.

Just off the foyer a well-appointed living room teams shades of khaki, blue, and orange. Subtle stripes, lighthearted patterns, and pretty florals willingly fuse with eighteenth-century antiques and Julian Schnabel's etching and aquatint *For Anna Magnani*, which dominates one wall. The doors in the living room are set low compared to the colossal recessed fireplace; the contrast in scale makes the proportions of the room seem grander than the actual dimensions would suggest. It is a counterpoint to their exotic, snug family room, the "Zam Zam" room, named after the mythical Islamic well. An antique, embroidered Indian fabric dramatically frames the door to the former service quarters above the garage. Leather poufs, along with Knoll tables and lounge chairs designed by Jens Risom, encircle the mirrored and Moroccan lattice-paneled fireplace. Puzzles and board games reside on the tables,

books line the built-in shelves, and photographs dot the space. It is unmistakably a room designed for comfort and lounging. A pair of fifteen-foot custom-made sofas is perfect for dogs, kids, watching movies, and sleepovers. Both Peter and Katie love all of the bric-a-brac that fills the space and the stories that go with the fanciful objects. They equally agree that their accumulated and diverse collections are what give the room a lively spirit. "We like uninhibited decorating that shows personality."

**DECORATIVE DETAILS** We look for poise and harmony in the connections between modern furnishings and great antiques. Embroidery and the needle arts are one of Katie's passions. From headboards to cushions, we have employed every embellishment imaginable in our home. Our dining room chairs are a great example. Red Thai silk and white appliquéd evil eyes, set against yellow upholstery and gray mohair, banish the idea that any room need be boring.

**FLOWERS AND FRAGRANCES** Garden roses, peonies, and dahlias are among our favorite flowers. We love their big, open blossoms and heady bouquets. Katie grows each variety in our garden, and we bring them into the house at every opportunity. We love all shades and color of flowers, yet gravitate toward an arrangement that has a beautiful scent. As for candles, Apothia Verde has a natural aroma that complements rather than competes with floral smells. Its spicy cilantro essence, mixed with notes of lime and chili, is wonderfully concentrated.

**A BEAUTIFUL BED** We use ivory cotton sheets with embroidered detail on the top sheet, and turn it down over a cotton pique blanket. A coverlet or blanket is usually tucked in with a down duvet at the foot of the bed folded in thirds so that it is easy to pull up when you get cold. Two king shams, two standard-size pillows, and one small decorative pillow (from back to front) top off the bedding. Never underestimate the transformative power of a great headboard. In our room, a green silk velvet Beckley bed provided us the perfect occasion to add more color and texture.

**ENTERTAINING THOUGHTS** Our preferred way to entertain is at home. The dining room is rarely a neglected and is often filled with family and friends. Peter usually cooks the dinner and I make dessert. Christmas, Thanksgiving, and Easter are our favorite holidays; especially when Peter makes Yorkshire pudding and roast beef with horseradish. In the summer, we switch gears and head to a small seaside town in Massachusetts, where Peter makes lobster risotto and I bake fresh rhubarb pie.

# KEVIN SHARKEY

STYLE IS SOMETHING THAT EVERYONE POSSESSES. DECIDING IF IT IS GOOD, BAD, IMPLEMENTED, OR IGNORED IS UP FOR DEBATE.

Kevin Sharkey can wax eloquent on any number of subjects. Art, entertaining, flowers, caviar, and the best uses for empty caviar tins are just a few topics that showcase his passions. Architecture and antiques motivate him as well, which stands to reason as he is senior vice president and executive editorial director of decorating for Martha Stewart Living Omnimedia. The Rhode Island School of Design graduate began his career with the venerable New York City interior design firm Parish-Hadley. In fact, it was Mr. Hadley himself who suggested that Kevin go to work for Martha. A traditionalist at heart, Kevin recently opted for a complete change when he moved into "a glass box in the sky" overlooking the Hudson River. The expansive apartment in New York City's West Village, designed by Richard Meier, is the antithesis of his previous homes. And yet he knew immediately it had the scale and proportion to be very glamorous and liveable.

The sun-filled space has almost 360-degree views of Manhattan, including the Hudson River and the Statue of Liberty. Not wanting to distract from the surrounding scenery or compete with the city outside his window, Kevin let the space "speak" to him and dictate the creative direction. Ultimately, he decided on midcentury modern furnishings, bold artwork, and a neutral color palette. This choice took him by surprise as "midcentury is not a language in which I am fluent," he admits. To bring his vision to life, furniture was kept low and the entire apartment (except for the kitchen) was painted the same color—walls, ceilings, woodwork, everything.

**DECORATIVE DETAILS** Although they are certainly not decorative, books and magazines bring my home to life, as does champagne, candy, music, and friends. I have champagne glasses of every incarnation and more iPods than any one person should be allowed to own. I also delight in the sound of laugher, and I smile every time I open the door to any one of my five godchildren.

Mirrors covering an entire wall of the living room thoughtfully reflect the river; the overall effect is soothing and seamless. Indulging his penchant for luxury, Kevin used silk carpeting, shearling rugs, and linen, velvet, and wool upholstery. An oak table stained the color of espresso coated with five layers of oil, gives the dining space a reflective quality. Delicately colored Chinese paper panels depicting flowers and birds further define the room. These panels have adorned the walls in all of his homes. Kevin's considered approach to design validates his conviction that a truly beautiful room is one that hasn't been "decorated," but rather one that has been considered. Decorating, he notes, is not about following preconceived rules. "You have to be inspired, passionate, and informed. Only then can you take a space and make it your own. That's really where beauty comes from—inside."

**MAKING AN ENTRANCE** I love my home, but the entryway was initially problematic. To overcome certain flaws, I furnished this space so that it functions perfectly. For practical purposes, there is a mirror, bench, console, and umbrella stand within immediate proximity of the coat closet. Fresh flowers and a pretty silver tray permanently reside on the console table—it is the first thing that people notice when they enter the space. Equally, I want guests to feel a true sense of welcome that only comes from a happy host.

**A BEAUTIFUL BED** I am very ascetic in the manner in which I sleep—no duvet or a million pillows for me. I want a bed that I can bounce a quarter off of, a nightstand with a bottle of water close by, and an open window regardless of season. I believe setting the perfect bed is all about the linens. In the winter, I use cashmere blankets and Portuguese flannel sheets in mint green, sky blue, pink, or butter yellow. I know it sounds very babyish, but the colors are very flattering. In the summer, I switch to white Irish linens with a heavy monogram. There are many days that I have gone to work with a "KJS" branded on my face in some unfortunate way.

**ENTERTAINING THOUGHTS** Spur-of-the-moment cocktail parties seem to work well in my apartment, with dinner parties coming in a close second. Manhattan by night provides a formidable and glamorous backdrop. I like to entertain all year long and I especially love holidays. I do not know how to cook, nor am I interested in learning, but I carefully consider every detail in organizing my gatherings. However, once I had to order last-minute pizza for a party and now it has become a tradition. My guests now know that the party isn't over if pizza has not been delivered. A friend once told me that if something isn't ready an hour before company arrives, don't worry about it. Just take a bath, have a drink, and await your guests. Everything sorts itself out in the end.

**FLOWERS AND FRAGRANCES** I am a complete slave to the seasons and welcome all four with open arms. My favorite flowers and foliage include tulips and pussy willows in the spring; peonies and gladiolas in the summer; dahlias and tall branches of colored leaves in the fall; amaryllis and all types of evergreens in the winter. My preferred flower, above all, is the carnation for its scent, form, and variety.

# SUZANNE AND CHRISTOPHER SHARP

## STYLE IS AN INDIVIDUAL AND ORIGINAL POINT OF VIEW DELIVERED WITH CONFIDENCE.

Suzanne and Christopher Sharp have an uncanny knack for turning the ordinary into the extraordinary. The founders of the Rug Company, Britain's bespoke rug retailer, have crafted a home and business that reflects their irreverent sense of humor and love of artistry. For the multicultural family (Suzanne was born in Malta and Christopher in Uganda), heirlooms and evocative antiques not only play an important role in their life but also bring much happiness and inspiration. Ideas for their rugs and designs often come from cultural aesthetics and found objects. "It can be the chaos of Palermo, the vitality of India, a jar from Tuscany, or the souks of Marrakech that trigger the imagination," says Suzanne. "All these experiences contribute to our visual vocabulary," adds Christopher. Over the last several years, the couple has collaborated with some of the best and brightest designers, including Alexander McQueen, Lulu Guinness, Nicky Haslam, Vivienne Westwood, Matthew Williamson, Diane von Furstenberg, and Paul Smith. The coveted rugs are featured in nearly every room of their house, along with quirky furnishings, flea-market finds, and jolts of bright color.

The rosy pink, bougainvillea-colored hallway is the first space to declare this is not the average Notting Hill Victorian house. A tarnished Union Jack flag in Aubusson wool, a Murano glass chandelier, vintage floral oil paintings, and antique gilded mirrors provide hints to what makes this couple tick. "We want a home that is modern, comfortable, and grounded," says Christopher. The vivacious parents of four children first met on the

**MAKING AN ENTRANCE** Our vibrant pink walls are a great contrast to the gray, gloomy London weather—they instantly lift the mood. A bespoke geometric rug running the whole length of the hall playfully leads you into the main rooms. For a bit of sparkle, we hung three oversized Tom Dixon silver ball lights. Each casts a welcoming glow, giving the space a strong identity.

London Underground and were married within a year. Their life together began with an extended backpacking honeymoon in India, followed by subsequent trips to remote locations and a brief stint living in the Middle East.

The duo is happiest at home sitting around the dining room table with family and friends. Christopher and Suzanne believe that little details matter most and have worked to create a happy and welcoming atmosphere. Care and consideration has been given to everything, from the quality of fabrics and the color of a vase to the aromatic scent of a candle. To keep their eyes fresh and home interesting, they like to move things around when the notion strikes. Both agree that the "rug" is a perfect example of their nomadic approach to decorating, and that their house is an ever-evolving expression of interests. "Our home is a continuous narrative. When the story ends, we move and start the next chapter."

**DECORATIVE DETAILS** An eclectic layering of patterns and prints is at the heart of our style and is present in each of our rooms. Salon-style hanging artwork and pictures are juxtaposed with boldly painted walls, whimsical tapestries, and colorful rugs. If we like something, we buy it. Predictability and fakery have no place in our home.

**FLOWERS AND FRAGRANCES** Log fires and flowers are a must in our home. Nothing compares to fresh flowers, especially 'Gertrude Jekyll' (a scented pink rose) and 'Madame Alfred Carrière' (a scented climbing cream-colored rose). Stiff-looking flowers are not our thing, but mixed bunches of green foliage, old-fashioned Baroness Rothschild roses, foxgloves, magnolia, and cherry blossoms are welcome in our home anytime. When we can't have the smell of a burning fire, Feu de Bois scented candles by Dyptique are amazing. For something wonderfully fresh, we like Jo Malone Basil and Verbena.

**A BEAUTIFUL BED** No clutter, a stack of good books, and a really thick pile rug (preferably pashmina) make the bedroom inviting—not stuffy. Good quality plain white linens, and pretty vintage pillowcases form the basis of our bed. We regularly change our bedspread for a different look. We have a lovely, cozy rabbit-fur throw for snowy wintery nights and Indian embroidered blankets for warmer months. There is something special about the ritual of changing your environment with the seasons.

**ENTERTAINING THOUGHTS** We love impromptu suppers in the kitchen, with guests of all ages enjoying good conversation, food, and wine. To make life easy, we keep a permanent drinks table set up at all times (ice bucket, mixers, spirits, wine, soft drinks, a variety of glasses, and nibbles). We never ever use plastic plates, paper cups, or paper napkins. Over the years, we've learned that candles, flowers, and good chocolates are essential treats for your guests. For an easy dinner, all you need is a good bottle of chilled wine, a big bowl of pasta, a green salad, some lovely cheeses, chocolate, and coffee.

# JAN SHOWERS

## I EQUATE STYLISH LIVING WITH A PERSONAL BLEND OF GRACE, KINDNESS, AND CHARM. STYLE SHOULD REFLECT A PERSON'S CHARACTER.

"Glamorous" and "comfortable" are adjectives often used to describe both Jan Showers's style and the rooms she fashions for clients. The words are certainly interchangeable in her vocabulary, but not mutually exclusive. "When I think of glamour, I don't think of Marie Antoinette in a corseted dress, but rather Grace Kelly in *Rear Window* or Audrey Hepburn in *Charade*." Movies, especially those from the 1940s, 1950s, and 1960s, inform her work and educate her eye. A modern nod to old Hollywood glamour forms the foundation of her interiors, with pale silks, sculptural lamps, and magnificent mirrors all playing a supporting role. A movie buff and Alfred Hitchcock aficionado, the composed blonde has made a name for herself well beyond the confines of her home state of Texas. The most spectacular examples of her efforts are her residences: a 1970s Dallas townhouse designed by Stanley Barrows, former director of interior design at Parsons School of Design, and a large 1930s Greek Revival family home just outside of the city.

It takes conviction, confidence, and Jan to combine warm silver-leafed ceilings with French parquet floors, Jansen chairs from the 1940s, Louis XV furniture upholstered in white cowhide, and sprinklings of vintage Murano glass. A long and ardent fan of mixing eighteenth- and nineteenth-century antiques with twentieth-century furniture, she is considered by many the doyenne of midcentury glamour. Jan has strong opinions about what constitutes comfort and glamour—upholstery must be luxurious, seating always comfortable, lamp lighting in every room (even outdoors), and tables within reach at all times. The result is liveable rooms and a well-edited accumulation of fabrics, antiques, and Moderne furnishings.

Liveability is always the most important element in the Showers equation. "I am somewhat subversive when it comes to trends," she admits, "I buck them at all cost." Another nonnegotiable in her decorating book is the use of rich paint colors. Deep platinum, green-tinted sea blues, and soft

**DECORATIVE DETAILS** Billy Baldwin once said, "A room is never successful if it's not personal." I truly believe that my personal collections bring our home to life; you instantly know that real people live here and love where they live. Books are such an important part of my world, and I stack them everywhere. Barware from the 1920s and 1930s, family photographs, fresh flowers, wonderful linens, china, and groupings of vintage Murano glass give our home a unique soul.

**ENTERTAINING THOUGHTS** I believe in
the word "dining." I would much rather dine
than eat. Seated dinner parties are my
preferred way of entertaining, and it's one of
the reasons that Thanksgiving is my favorite
holiday. Not only for the wonderful tradition,
but also the opportunity to have my entire
family gather at the table. I think that eight
people for a dinner party is a perfect number
(ten at most). If we are having eight people or
fewer, I will serve dinner in the living room
using the banquette for seating. I try to do as
much as possible ahead of time so that I can
enjoy my company. A relaxed hostess and
simply prepared food will always be a hit. And
never underestimate the splendor of serving
drinks in pretty stemware (everything looks
more tempting in a martini glass), and a
beautifully set table makes food taste better.

tones of aubergine wash the walls of her homes, and she swears by Donald Kaufman wall paint for its elegant luster.

Blending the past with the present seems to come easy and naturally for Jan. However, she insists there is no magic formula and is quick to point out many happy "accidents" that have occurred along the way. As an interior designer, she believes the past informs the present, and like many she draws inspiration from her predecessors, including Billy Baldwin, Frances Elkins, and David Hicks. "The living room Billy Baldwin did for Mary Wells Lawrence at La Fiorentina in the South of France will forever live in my memory. Billy embodied clean, simple glamour." Jan has her own knack for finding beauty in the simplest of details and is happiest reading, watching old movies with her husband, Jim, or sitting by the fire sipping a drink. I think Dallas-based writer Rebecca Sherman summed it up best when she wrote, "A serene Grace Kelly in *To Catch a Thief* might have been Jan Showers's perfect client."

**MAKING AN ENTRANCE** Understated glamour is at the heart of my design philosophy and personal style. I love beautiful clothes and objects, but I also want to look and feel relaxed. I'm not a buttoned-up kind of girl, and I find a little element of surprise goes a long way. I like a bit of the unexpected when you open the door to a home, and I adhere to these same principles when I create an entryway. In our Dallas townhouse, I lined the walls with warm silver tea paper, brought in a mirrored commode, and added soft lamplight. It's simple yet glamorous. It's not what you would expect when walking into a townhouse built in the 1970s. The space always glows and gives off a warm and intimate feeling.

**A BEAUTIFUL BED** I adore nothing more than creating a luxurious bed for both sleeping and reading. Reading is vital to my life, not only for learning but also relaxing. That is why eye-level lighting is so important, along with a convenient

bedside table that doubles as a bookcase. My favorite linens are Sferra percale. Cool cotton percale sheeting is perfect for living in Texas. On the occasion it does turn cold, I top the bed with a lightweight cotton blanket. I prefer to keep my bed simple, but will bring in texture and color by using a Raoul Textile decorative pillow.

**FLOWERS AND FRAGRANCES** I love the associations and memories that come with certain fragrances. Purple hyacinths bring me pure joy for both their scent and sight. The smell of hyacinths always reminds me of spring and Easter. Dahlias are another favorite. They are so incredibly beautiful that they almost appear unreal. I relish looking at them loosely arranged in one of my Murano glass vases. Guerlain's L'Heure Bleue will forever carry me back to the fall when I first met my husband. I still wear it to this day. I must admit that I am not big on scented candles, and I feel that they are overused.

# MATTHEW PATRICK SMYTH

## STYLE IS THE METHOD OF DEFINING WHO WE ARE AND HOW WE LIVE.

Matthew Patrick Smyth lives an enviable life. During the week, he resides on the Upper East Side of Manhattan and on the weekends he shares a home in Sharon, Connecticut, with his longtime partner, French author Jean Vallier. The couple also keep apartments in Paris and Palm Beach. However, it is their late eighteenth-century colonial farmhouse, in the peaceful hamlet of Litchfield County, where they escape most often. Matthew first discovered the property while searching the Internet for a rural retreat within easy reach of New York. The main part of the house, built in 1790, endured many "bad" additions and renovations over the years. For a spell, it was an inn for lady schoolteachers before coming into Matthew's care.

While the house was in need of repair, as with any renovation, there are always surprises and frustrations. Matthew even questioned his own judgment at one point during the chaotic process. A few discoveries that brought delight were a concealed Palladian window and a hidden tiger-maple staircase with ivory inlay, features that had been closed off by previous owners. What gave him further pleasure was an engraved brass chime on the door dated September 8, 1884, the same day as his birthday (minus a hundred-plus years).

After a five-month-long structural renovation, Matthew turned his attention to the interior spaces. Furniture from a former home was moved in, along with collections and objects from the many showhouse rooms he created over the years. Floorboards were painted black to create a unified look and mirrors artfully placed to reflect light and amplify space. A mirror

**CREATURE COMFORTS** Coming home to comfortable seating with a good reading light, a table at hand for books, glasses (both reading and drinking), and a good stereo is heaven. And the days that I have no set schedule, when I am free to read, nap, putter, and just enjoy my home, are pure bliss.

per room is one of his favorite design rules; it not only directs his thinking but also forces consideration from every angle. "Of course, you can have more than just one mirror in a room," he notes. "Practically speaking, it's imperative to consider what the first mirror will do before even contemplating adding a second."

It is the same intense focus that drives his every decision. The interior designer originally thought he would be a photographer. "I didn't know I could be a decorator. In my tiny hometown of Florida, New York, there were no decorators." It was only after meeting a designer and watching Dick Cavett interview Katharine Hepburn that Matthew changed his path. The famous actress declared that you could have anything you want in life if you narrowed your focus; if not you would never

**DECORATIVE DETAILS** Never underestimate the power of flowers. Rooms move into another realm when you introduce real flowers and plants. Any item or object that you take care in finding, regardless of cost, adds uniqueness and soul. I always search out things that both amuse and delight. I hate it when music is missing from my home, and I will never forgo light-bulb control. Dimmers are essential.

go anywhere. Soon after he narrowed his focus and pursued a career in design, attending the Fashion Institute of Technology, he then worked for David Easton, his chosen mentor. Much like Mr. Easton, Matthew's work is grounded in tradition, but he has loosened up over the years, now freely mixing twentieth-century pieces with antiques. He doesn't like rooms that are too studied. Nor does he care for gimmicks. Moreover, he credits travel with widening his design views and ideas. "I can work seven days a week for months if I know a trip is coming up to renew my senses. Travel turns me on creatively, spiritually, and emotionally."

**MAKING AN ENTRANCE** It all begins and ends at the front door. Therefore, it's important to spend some time and care in thinking about not only beautiful decoration, but also the functional design of the space. A place to sit and remove winter boots is a must in our home. A forgiving carpet, sturdy umbrella stand, and easy access to a coat closet are also important. Naturally, the imperative details vary greatly depending on the home and locale.

**FLOWERS AND FRAGRANCES** The fresh scent of Antica Farmacista's Green Fig is one of my favorites. In the winter, I sometimes use their Pomegranate & Currant, a warm, spicy aroma blended with citrus. Of course, I am always open to new scents, especially when given as a gift. White tulips are simple and elegant flowers for the home, and in my garden everything is white or blue. I like the clean, crisp look of those colors mixed with green; it's visually less confusing.

**A BEAUTIFUL BED** A fairly simple bed, with four pillows stacked two by two, a top sheet, and a folded duvet, works for me. Pressed linens are wonderful, but the reality of servicing them is an issue. I am always on the lookout for the finest no-iron sheets and pillowcases. The best I have found are Land's End 400-count embroidered sateen sheets. They have a pressed appearance right from the dryer. The linens in our house are not necessarily changed out with the seasons, but the duvet cover, quilts, and blankets do reflect the time of year.

**ENTERTAINING THOUGHTS** When I am in the city, I like to take small groups of friends to Off Broadway shows at the Irish Repertory Theatre or Classic Stage Company; we always have drinks and light food beforehand at a nearby restaurant. I find that December is the easiest month for entertaining at home. Everyone is in a festive mood, decorations are more creative, and anything seems to go. When pressed for time, I buy dessert and order appetizers from a Turkish restaurant.

# CHRISTOPHER SPITZMILLER

## STYLISH LIVING IS SURROUNDING YOURSELF WITH PERSONAL OBJECTS THAT HAVE BEEN EDITED IN A VISUALLY PLEASING WAY.

Ceramist Christopher Spitzmiller's impassioned pursuit for creating hand-thrown, highly glazed colorful lamps has created a cult following among designers and design aficionados. Off-white vellum paper shades, perched atop gilt bases outfitted with jewel-like hardware, possess artful sophistication. His exacting creations can be found in homes and rooms ranging from the Oval Office to the United States Consulate General's residence in Ho Chi Minh City. Christopher's career began near Georgetown, Washington, D.C., where he set up a studio in an old schoolhouse. In the summers, he worked at Mecox Gardens in Southampton, New York, as an artist-in-residence. Before long, many respected designers, including Albert Hadley, Richard Keith Langham, and Suzanne Rheinstein, commissioned his work, which prompted him to move to New York City and start a full-time business.

If you believe that good things come in pairs, Christopher's home brims with greatness. Inspired by the yellow living room of Evangeline Bruce, the elegant wife of the former United States envoy to France, egg-yolk-colored glazed walls welcome frequent guests as do his dogs, Happy and Suzy. Lamps in Prussian blue illuminate either side of the sofa, a pair of oval painted medallions (formerly belonging to Mrs. Bruce) hang suspended from the crown molding, two Regency chairs from Pamela Harriman's estate flank the fireplace, and two small watercolors by Mark Hampton rest on the bookcase. The designer gravitates toward orderly, symmetrical arrangements anchored by a strong focal point. The balance allows him to indulge in his passion for beautiful objects without overpowering the small space.

The rich and vibrant palette of his ground-floor apartment ranges from exquisitely dark walnut to deep apple green. A fan of traditional design and old-school charm, he manages to keep a lighthearted hold on his "homey" style. "It's a slightly modernized version of Colefax and Fowler." Friends Todd Romano and the late Albert Hadley both played a role in helping the potter bring his design vision into being. Several

**FLOWERS AND FRAGRANCES**

Anemones are my favorite flower. Luckily, I found a grower in Rhinebeck, New York, that will send them FedEx from Labor Day right through Mother's Day. In the spring, I bring in Sir Winston Churchill narcissus that I grow in my country garden; and in the summer, I cut sweet peas for arrangements. I always have a candle burning, and I cycle through different scents with the seasons. Right now I am fond of the Thé candle from Todd Romano.

of his ideas and possessions came from auctions, old auction catalogs, and flea markets. In the square entry hall, a mirrored front door reflects a shell-encrusted Parsons table found in a Southampton thrift store, a mirror by Bill Sullivan purchased on the suggestion of Mr. Hadley, a loop chair by Frances Elkins, and a Van Day Truex painting entitled *The Shells of Boca Grande*.

The Upper East Side apartment was originally two townhouses built in 1910, later joined together and split up into smaller units. Positioned in the far rear of the building is a small garden—a true luxury in New York. Ferns, climbing ivy, and blooming hellebores thrive in large planters. A gravel path leads to white wrought-iron chairs and a small sitting area. The upside is of course privacy, a place to entertain, and no waiting for an elevator. The downside of the ground-floor flat is a lack of natural light. "Every morning I have to turn on several of my lamps. That's the life of a lamp maker."

**MAKING AN ENTRANCE** My dogs always welcome me home. They both come dancing forward with their tails wagging, as if to say, "You're here! You're here! Welcome home!" It's such a good feeling and I try to pass on their enthusiasm to all of my friends. Sentiments aside, my Benjamin Moore Maritime Blue entryway never grows old. It's a welcoming, soft blue-green shade that I use everywhere. If I could be a color, this would be the one—it's cool and calming.

**DECORATIVE DETAILS** I like seeing some of the stains that life leaves behind. A slightly unfinished baseboard, layers of paint with some visible cracks, and paw marks on the painted floors—all showcase a home that is loved and lived in. Keith Irving once said that he liked rugs so threadbare you might not be able to walk across them. That's taking it a little far, but I see his point.

**A BEAUTIFUL BEDROOM** I am a "sheetaholic." There are countless sets of sheets in my linen closet. I am on a first-name basis with Carol at Porthault in New York. I also adore Jane Scott Hodges's Leontine Linens. Jane Scott has created some wonderful monogrammed antique linen French sheets and pillowcases for me. She is truly the best at monograms. I like bedding that is well worn; both cotton percale and linen sheets need a lot of washing and ironing to acquire the right feel. I love to buy new sheets, but like shoes, they need to be broken in to achieve the ultimate comfort.

**ENTERTAINING THOUGHTS** Dinner parties are my favorite way to entertain, but I have given up on the idea that I can run a business and cook dinner. I set the table the night before and make part of the meal myself ahead of time (usually dessert). My sister recently gave me an ice-cream maker. I love that I can make ice cream over the weekend and have part of the meal done. For the rest, I call a local restaurant and have them deliver. It takes the stress out of entertaining, making me a much better host.

# MADELINE STUART
## STYLE IS BEAUTY WITHOUT PRETENSE.

Armed with a quick smile and infectious charm, Madeline Stuart is both smart and wonderfully straightforward. She speaks her mind in a way that is refreshing and draws on a deep knowledge of her craft. Growing up in Beverly Hills with a film director father and a mother who is an interior designer, she developed an early appreciation for books, movies, and beautiful surroundings. In fact, as a ten-year-old bibliophile she inspired her father to create the classic 1971 movie *Willy Wonka and the Chocolate Factory*. Mel Stuart had never read Roald Dahl's novel *Charlie and the Chocolate Factory*, but Madeline loved it and wanted to see it on the big screen. "I knew it would be a great motion picture. So I asked him to make it," she recalls.

Madeline is a person who trusts her creative instincts, especially when it comes to architecture and interior design. She and her husband, writer Steve Oney, live in a classic 1930s red-tile-roof Spanish Revival home perched high in the Hollywood Hills. Stucco walls, handcrafted beams, wrought-iron railings, small terraces, and built-in alcoves are just a few of the distinctive hallmarks of the architecture that enjoyed great popularity in California between 1915 and 1931. Their house is one of the original properties in Outpost Estates, the former hunting grounds for General Harrison Gray Otis, the influential early publisher of the *Los Angeles Times*. Touted as the "jewel in the hills" by its developer, the area reflects a glamorous bygone era with splendid single-family homes set on vast lots with astounding views. Even today the neighborhood is still relatively rustic. "We are just a few blocks north of Hollywood

**CREATURE COMFORTS** It's important to be surrounded by beautiful things—not necessarily expensive things, just ones that are well chosen. Comfortable furniture and wonderful places to sit and read are a key requirement. I also love cooking in the kitchen while my husband sits and talks or reads to me. It's very centering.

## MAKING AN ENTRANCE

I hope that everyone who walks
through my front door
immediately gets my style, sense
of humor, and sensibility. I
want our house to be
welcoming and intriguing all at
the same time. I love it when
people come in, wander around,
and study the collected objects.

Boulevard and we have coyotes, bobcats, and deer roaming the streets," says Madeline.

The union of architectural integrity and beauty is apparent the moment you step inside the heavy wooden door. The interiors are carefully edited, serenely contemporary, and retain many features original to the house. "Historical honesty is important to me, but I wouldn't describe myself as a slave to the period. Nor do I think the interior of our home is truly decorated. The look is more suggestive of furnishings and objects that we have assembled over time." Madeline is a firm believer that good design comprises the objects, artwork, and furnishings that reflect and respect the people who live in a house. These attributes are apparent in her home. A side terrace, with views of the garden, is a tranquil spot for relaxing, reading, and watching Beatrice, her beloved Jack Russell, chase lizards. "I am happiest outside with a book, newspapers, and pile of magazines by my side. It's one of the few opportunities I have for peace and quiet."

**DECORATIVE DETAILS** Certainly books are high on my list, but not for purely decorative purposes. The time I spend at home reading is highly valued and adds much meaning to my life. I don't understand grouping and displaying books because the spines match. It's completely absurd. Nor do I like accessories that clearly have been chosen by a decorator, as it looks too contrived. A collection of consequential bits and pieces is equally comforting and essential.

**FLOWERS AND FRAGRANCES** I adore lavender and citrus, both in raw form and candles. In winter months, I like tobacco and leather scents. I am not a fan of those sticks that come out of a jar, and I don't really care for potpourri of any kind. I favor peonies for their beauty and poppies for their colors and shapes. In my own garden, I don't have any flowers, only plants and shrubs.

**A BEAUTIFUL BED** Once I was obsessed with vintage linens, but now I use only sateen sheets on my bed. No top sheet, just down pillows and a duvet. Living in Los Angeles, I rarely change my linens with the season. In the winter, I will add a blanket at the bottom of the bed. Good reading lights, open windows, our dog, and a lavender sachet next to my pillow provide the essentials for a great bedroom.

**ENTERTAINING THOUGHTS** I have a few simple rules for entertaining. No paper or plastic. Ever. And I always serve plenty of alcohol. Fall and winter months provide a great opportunity to gather around the fireplace. Unless you live on the coast, it's just too darn hot to have a roaring fire most months out of the year, so I try and make the most of cool weather. I adore having friends over for dinner, but I am not very good at the drop-by- or stop-by-for-a drink thing. I wish I were better at simple entertaining, but I'm not sure that it's in my DNA.

# ROSE TARLOW

## MANY HOMES ARE PERFECTLY DESIGNED BUT THEY FAIL TO REFLECT THE PERSONALITIES OF THE PEOPLE WHO LIVE THERE. THE ABSENCE IS DISTURBINGLY VISIBLE.

Rose Tarlow's Bel Air home is the embodiment of imagination and natural beauty. Creeping vines from the home's exterior cascade down twenty-foot interior walls in her sun-dappled living room and wind around eighteenth-century French doors; a look that she both conceived and encouraged. It is with a rigorous and discerning eye and a keen understanding of proportion that she makes her every decision. She is driven and precise and does not conform to accepted rules or standards. "I see what is necessary and eliminate useless details."

Many speak of homes that are timeless, but few go to the painstaking effort to create such a place. Out of a desire to prove to herself that designing an ageless house was, in fact, possible, Rose set out to craft a masterpiece along a quiet wooded canyon, and filled it with the characteristics of an Old World structure. Drawn to rooms with high ceilings and dark wood beams, she studied the homes built by Wallace Neff, one of California's most distinguished and influential architects. Salvaged materials and old woods were shipped in from Europe. Crossbeams in the living room, from an eleventh-century English church, now add the perfect patina, while seventeenth-century oak wood covers the floors. In the dining room and kitchen, old stone pavers from France lie underfoot, the master bedroom is anchored by French pine boiserie, and a circular staircase found in a Paris flea market climbs to a sleeping alcove in her art studio.

Every object and piece of furniture in her home tells its own story. As a result, each room has a distinct personality. In the living room, a large drawing by Jean Cocteau hangs above a massive stone fireplace (one of two in the room), and a seventeenth-century Knole sofa retains its original worn velvet and detailed embroidery. "Creating a home is like writing a book. First you create characters and then you tell a story. When you finish, it no longer belongs to you. It becomes a living thing that others enjoy."

**DECORATIVE DETAILS** Open windows, the scent of fresh air and flowers, good lighting, and a feeling that everything is clean and crisp are important and fundamental details. All of these things, along with my treasures and books, offer a prevailing sense of peace at home. Furniture and accessories must be considered with great care and attention. If my rooms were food, they would be something delightfully comforting like macaroni and cheese with a crusty top.

The same singular vision and design philosophy lies at the heart of her Los Angeles–based company, Rose Tarlow Melrose House. Renowned for its furniture, each piece is a reinterpretation of classic antiques, as well as its more modern designs that are crafted by the same local artisans Rose has used for years. French, English, and Asian influences exquisitely complement her choice of materials—metal, wood, aged leather, and worn silk velvet. "Everything you live with should be wonderful and of great quality—not necessarily expensive, just very good."

**ENTERTAINING THOUGHTS** If you entertain regularly, it is so much easier than doing it rarely. If you are well prepared, each occasion becomes a wonderful variation on a familiar theme. My favorite times of year are deep winter and deep summer. I like to serve cozy dinners in front of a fire when the days turn cold, and dine outside when the weather permits it. Usually, I will only have a few cool people around that I really enjoy, and who make me laugh.

**MAKING AN ENTRANCE** An entryway is like the opening chapter of a book; it lures you in and welcomes you to a world beyond the front door. As well, it should speak volumes about those who live in the house. I love and appreciate my home, and I want for that to come across to all who enter my private space.

**FLOWERS AND FRAGRANCES** I love my Melrose House candles year-round. However, in the winter, nothing is better than the smell of a wonderful fire burning in the fireplace, and during the spring and summer, I crave the scent of fresh lavender and lily of the valley. As for flowers, I gravitate towards white daffodils, tuberoses, and cut branches from the trees in my garden.

**A BEAUTIFUL BED** I prefer a bed that is simply set. I use crisp, pure linen sheets in the winter and high-quality cotton in the summer months. I favor white linen pillows and sheets, topped with a satin or cotton coverlet. A warm, heavily scented bath before I lie down to sleep in a freshly made bed is the perfect way to end the day.

# COLETTE VAN DEN THILLART

EFFORTLESS STYLE IS A LIE. IT TAKES
A GREAT DEAL OF ENTHUSIASM, DETERMINATION,
AND HARD WORK TO HAVE STYLE.

A versatile mix of people and places are essential to the multifaceted life of Colette van den Thillart. The edgy, witty, and confident creative director of Nicky Haslam Design is the perfect complement to the iconic founder who bears the company name. For the past few years, Colette and her family have divided time between London and Barbados; most recently they added Toronto to the list when she was appointed to oversee Nicky Haslam Design North America. While each of her homes is intensely personal and idiosyncratic to its locale, Colette took cues from her self-appointed design family (Dorothy Draper, John Fowler, Elsie de Wolfe, Nancy Lancaster, David Hicks, and Tony Duquette) when plotting plans for her most recent house. "You need a bit of everything—high, low, beautiful, homely, grand, and always a little something to make you laugh." The rooms are light and airy with touches of dramatic color, romantic fabrics, and overscaled furniture. Polished silver, rich shades of blue, and brushed gold spring to life against pristine white living room walls—a nod to Elsie de Wolfe, who believed in white paint. Snippets of poems, hand-painted by Colette onto ornately framed canvases, pay homage to Ms. Draper, who famously used opulent plaster moldings in her designs. "I wanted this house to have a sense of flamboyance and grandeur," says Colette. "But at the end of the day, it's a comfortable family home."

Driven by an international viewpoint and eclectic sensibility, the "closet historian" feels strongly that rooms, including contemporary ones, should have emotional layers. "I don't much care for houses that look like hotels. Perhaps such rooms look attractive in photographs, but where are the books or the personalities?" she asks. Like many designers, it is the unexpected visual moments (a single taper candle burning in the window, a sculpture intended for the garden placed on a hall table, or an array of complex colors) that drive and inspire her aesthetics. In addition to Colette's "design family," other inspirers

**DECORATIVE DETAILS** Color is key to setting the mood you desire and proper furniture placement is paramount. Everything in my home must "speak" to one another and make me smile. I adore creating vignettes and tablescapes with all of the things that I collect and cherish. I am forever moving stuff around to match my mood or season. In every room, I want at least one insanely swoon-worthy object, plus my treasured books and ephemera from loved ones.

include eighteenth-century architects Claude Nicolas Ledoux and Étienne-Louis Boullée; film directors Federico Fellini and David Lynch; and artists David LaChapelle and Cy Twombly. These creative individuals sustain her belief that a room should be open to influence while mixing fascinating one-of-a-kind finds with simpler pieces.

Incandescent lighting, candles, fires, steam showers, heated floors, sound insulation, solid wood doors, and a close connection to the garden are among her prerequisites for an inspiring home. And while designing rooms that "quietly haunt" and "delight" are Colette's ultimate goal, in the end it is about creating enchanting spaces that allow people to feel uplifted.

**MAKING AN ENTRANCE** I like entryways that are stimulating, glamorous, and offer an element of surprise—but nothing too trite or overt. There should be a certain level of simplicity and romance that compels you to pause and anticipate all that is to come. When I arrive home, I feel alive, loved, and inspired. I want my home to put others in the same frame of mind.

**FLOWERS AND FRAGRANCES** I grew up with four very distinct seasons and respond to each so differently. Every season has its own visual and sensual flowers and foliage, but the peony is my favorite. With all flowers, I crave shades of white, pink, violet, and green. Sometimes I will create arrangements exclusively with green hues. The effect is stunning. White is the most wonderfully academic of all colors, soft pink provides a visual pause, and violet is almost transcendental. Until ten years ago, I very rarely used scents in my home, but now I am drawn to the earthy smells of salt, wax, tobacco, pepper, and woodsmoke found in Frederic Malle's Dans Tes Bras.

**A BEAUTIFUL BED** Folded-back bedding with one corner tugged down in a beckoning manner is my idea of heaven. I want a bed that is not too perfect and has had a chance to breathe. My husband and I are on different thermostats so we have a silk summer duvet and also an enormous down duvet. It gives the bed a delightful, billowy look. At night, we climb in and tug our own "layer" upon us. Rarely do I change linens with the seasons. I am a fan of the white, crisp percale sheets infused with ironing water. Some of my beds have embroidered accents, and I do tend to add blankets across the bottom in colder months. I am a bit of a blanket addict and cannot get enough of the layered look.

**ENTERTAINING THOUGHTS** I always cook and decorate the table in accordance with the season. As for guests, I mix the very young, for their beauty and energy, with the old, for their intellect and wit. Summer seems most conducive to spontaneity and gaiety. When we are in Barbados, I set the table with great effort, but display a sort of irreverence toward the food. Once summer comes to an end, I long for intimate late-night winter dinners in my London dining room with old-fashioned classics on the table—beouf bourguignon is a favorite. The walls of the dining room are lined with books and the only source of light comes from candles. It's very dramatic and glamorous—everyone looks divine!

# MATTHEW WHITE

I LIKE TO SURROUND MYSELF WITH FRIENDS, FAMILY,
BELOVED PETS, GOOD FOOD, AND BOOKS. ALL OF THESE ELEMENTS
ARE ESSENTIAL TO LIVING AND BRING GREAT JOY TO MY LIFE.

Interior designer Matthew White is living proof that beauty is not where we find it, it's where we make it—no matter how modest our beginnings. Growing up in Amarillo, Texas, Matthew had a happy but humble childhood. He spent much time reading *Better Homes & Gardens*, drawing, and helping his family beautify their parcel of land at the Tumbleweed Trailer Park. Inspired by the knowledge that "elbow grease and a little gumption" could transform any space, he decided at the age of seven that he wanted to one day become an interior designer. Though not a common trade for a boy growing up in the Texas Panhandle, he had the full support of his family.

Before he fully immersed himself in the world of design, he bucked tradition by pursuing a career in dance at the prestigious School of American Ballet in New York City. Not giving up on his love of interiors, however, he helped support his training by working at an antiques shop, where he learned about period styles. After years of dancing professionally with the Los Angeles Ballet, he opened Matthew White Antiques & Interiors in Pasadena, California. It was during this time that he and his partner, Broadway producer Thomas Schumacher, began their love affair with historic preservation by restoring old houses.

After renovating several properties, and following a life-changing trip to Italy, Matthew and Thomas found their dream home—a 1924 Italian Revival house they named Villa delle Favole, the "House of Myths and Fairy Tales." The villa had fallen victim to poor renovations and neglect over several years, but Matthew and Thomas lovingly brought the house and its historic garden back to life. Not long after, the two were introduced to Save

**CREATURE COMFORTS** I adore good food and am happiest when sitting at the dining table and sharing a meal that has been lovingly prepared. Napping on the sofa with our dachshund, Holden, is also sheer joy. A house without life is not a home. Our dog and my beloved are what give our home life meaning. Of course, books, art, and plenty of chocolate make me very happy, too.

Venice, Inc., an American nonprofit organization that restores art and monuments in the ancient city on the Adriatic. To help with these efforts, Matthew offered to design and host a masked ball in the extensive gardens of their villa. The party was an amazing success, attracting designers, artists, and jet-setters from all over the world. The event not only raised much-needed funds but it also launched the California chapter of Save Venice, Inc.

Thomas's production role with Disney necessitated a move to Manhattan and once again they were in search of a place that would house their growing collection of Italian furniture and art. An apartment in the historic 1891 Robb House, designed by McKim, Mead & White, fit the bill perfectly; however, like their former home, it was in need of

**MAKING AN ENTRANCE** When I walk into my home, I feel as if I have entered the happiest place on earth. I like simple entrances that slowly lead one into a house. I often look to the older homes of Italy or France for inspiration. At first glance, those entry halls may appear to be sedate or even austere, but that's what makes stepping into the grand, public rooms all the more pleasurable.

Matthew's design vision and preservation skills. The space was fraught with unfortunate decisions from previous renovations such as misplaced bookshelves and a poorly placed staircase. After restoring the historic rooms and reimagining the nonhistoric ones, the space was returned to its former glory.

On the weekends, the two escape to an Italian-inspired twenty-first-century villa they built in the Hudson Valley. Though very different in style, both of their homes evoke Italy, a sense of history and romance entwined with comfortable furnishings, intriguing objects, and interesting art. For Matthew, comfort is of the utmost importance for people and pets alike. Appropriateness and harmony are also design qualities that he admires and employs in his work and daily life. Overly "serious" rooms turn him off emotionally, as does money poorly spent, whether it's a little or a lot. "It doesn't take much money to choose quality," he notes, "but it does take knowledge." Matthew continues to live by a strong work ethic and the words of George Balanchine: "First comes the sweat, then comes the beauty if you're very lucky and have said your prayers."

**DECORATIVE DETAILS** Accessories that have no history or are created simply for decorative purposes hold no interest for me. When carefully chosen, they give a room texture and detail. I particularly love old handmade objects that tell a story. Venetian glass is pure magic. Not only does it remind me of my favorite city but it is also an ancient applied art. Likewise I'm drawn to sculptures carved from stone or wood for their beauty and natural quality.

**FLOWERS AND FRAGRANCES** There is nothing better than the smell of a truly clean house, enhanced by fresh flowers or the organic essence of a candle. Synthetic fragrances are like air pollution. Lilacs and garden roses possess a heavenly scent and are among my favorite flowers. I also love fresh herbs picked right from the garden. Few things are more appetizing than a big bunch of fresh-cut basil in the kitchen.

**A BEAUTIFUL BED** I like a bed to be properly made each day. Turning down the bed at night is like a beautiful woman taking down her hair. And although I like a bed that is properly made, I prefer for it to be done in a simple manner with not too many pillows, adequate blankets, and a bedspread to cover it all up. Crisp cotton sheets that have been beautifully pressed, down pillows, and a soft blanket create the perfect nest for slumber.

**ENTERTAINING THOUGHTS** I am passionate about entertaining. Each season is filled with reasons to gather together, and I like them all— weekend breakfasts, lunch in the garden with a crisp cold rosé, multiple-course dinners by candlelight, or afternoon tea. I always prefer simple food that suits the season, and I don't much care for overwrought table decor. Simplicity is more pleasing to the eye. Nothing lifts the spirit like seeing a table blazing with candles once dinner is called. It's a magical moment.

# HUTTON WILKINSON
### STYLE IS A PERSONAL STATEMENT
### THAT REFLECTS HOW YOU LIVE, ENTERTAIN,
### AND DRESS FOR EVERY OCCASION.

Hutton Wilkinson is a modern-day Renaissance gentleman with a manic schedule. He thrives on creative energy, imaginative ideas, and interesting people. Yet, he is never too busy to stay in touch with friends, host lavish parties, raise funds for favorite charities, build a new home, design jewelry, lighting, furniture, and fabrics, and oversee the iconic Dawnridge estate, former home of his late business partner, legendary designer Tony Duquette. One of America's design icons, Duquette, who was discovered by the great decorator Lady Elsie de Wolfe Mendl, was mentor and friend to Hutton for more than thirty years. Following Duquette's passing in 1999, Hutton became owner and president of Tony Duquette, Inc. Wishing to preserve the historic property, Hutton and his wife, Ruth, purchased the fabled Beverly Hills residence to use as a "party house" and "office" (in that order). Wilkinson's most recent home, Casa la Condessa, is the latest addition to the legendary Dawnridge property.

With "sideways" entries and all principal rooms facing south, the new dwelling was based on Charlestonian-style houses. The layout and prime position afford all who enter fabulous views of the neighboring garden and reflecting lake.

**CREATURE COMFORTS** Books, old porcelain, down pillows, good reading light, a long sofa to stretch out on, and a television set tuned to Turner Classic Movies are just a few of the things I crave in life. I adore hot, hot, hot food—both spicy hot and hot with heat—hot fudge sauce, a box of caramels sprinkled with sea salt, and a very deep tub brimming with a lot of hot water. Last, but certainly not least, friends (lots of friends). I like a cast of thousands around me, although my wife would prefer to be a hermit. I need all of this and more for my physical well-being and happiness.

The street-level front doors open onto an expansive black marble foyer, with a balcony overlooking a double-height drawing room. "The property is basically a ravine and I love that you can look down into the drawing room from the hallway, dining room, library, and stairwell. It is exactly how I like it— one-room living." Devoid of fussy architectural details, Hutton created a blank canvas and stage for his exuberant lifestyle and many moods. Think Auntie Mame. "If I want the house to be Venetian today and Chinese tomorrow, nothing stands in my way."

The entire abode was designed to display his beloved Venetian paintings that once belonged to Baroness Catherine d'Erlanger. The paintings, along with his family's South American heirlooms, portraits, and coats of arms, are the "decorative punctuation marks" among many treasures. They are also the very belongings that make him smile each day. "Unfortunately, all of this happiness has turned me into a veritable recluse and I find that I must almost force myself to go out and see what's happening in the world." Fortunately, the world seems to seek out Hutton. A coveted invitation from the consummate host

is like a golden ticket. The place is tailor-made for entertaining, which Hutton does often, greeting guests in a full silk robe while offering Champagne, with his wife, Ruth, by his side. "Here's the deal. You can have the most beautiful and most stylish interiors in all the world, but if you don't know how to live in your home, how to entertain, how to dress for the occasion, or how to fill it with the right people (that is to say, like-minded people who will understand your personal statement), then you've only got part of the equation right."

**MAKING AN ENTRANCE** An entrance hall sets the mood and tone for all that is to come. I think it is the most important room of all. At our house, the entrance starts outside, just beyond a tall black iron gate. The minute you enter the front courtyard you can see through the glass front doors all the way through the house to the back courtyard. Both the front and back gardens are lit with gaslights, offering a soft glow and welcoming flicker. Our house exudes warmth (literally and figuratively). Radiant heat warms the marble floors and softly scented incense envelops all who enter. Whenever I come home, I have an immense feeling of expectancy and anticipation, like lighting candles before a festival.

**FLOWERS AND FRAGRANCES** I haven't the time or the inclination to be fussing over the arrangement of flowers. I usually lean toward growing plants or potted flowers. It's one of the reasons that I like flowering orchids; they are easy and pretty. I adore gardenias and China lilies for their aroma and appearance. China lilies are especially beautiful when planted in antique blue-and-white Canton cachepots. All of my friends know to give me Rigaud candles—they are the best.

**A BEAUTIFUL BED** I love daybeds for a dressing room. But in the bedroom, I must have a canopy bed, the taller the better. If I can't have a bed with really tall posts, then I want fabulous fabric hung from the ceiling in David Hicks style. I like to change my linens all the time (not just with the season), and I am crazy for beautiful colors and patterns. The more linens in the linen closet the better. Give me embroidered or printed cotton percale and a thin blanket any day. For the perfect foundation, I desire very firm mattresses. Although I could happily sleep on top of a billiard table.

**ENTERTAINING THOUGHTS** Ruth and I host lunch for four to eight people every day and we invite guests on Wednesday nights. While at our place in Malibu, we only host lunch when we have houseguests. We revel in Easter Sunday brunch, Thanksgiving dinner (served at a normal eight o'clock hour), Christmas Eve dinner, and New Year's Day lunch (always alfresco). We expect our guests to dress for the occasion, but for Christmas Eve, black tie is de rigueur. If the weather is particularly hot, which it can be in Los Angeles, then I like to wear fabulous pajamas to my parties, but that's my thing. My friends say I'm the only person they know that goes directly from pajamas to bed clothes without having to change.

# BUNNY WILLIAMS

## STYLE IS HAVING THE CREATIVITY AND IMAGINATION TO MAKE YOUR SURROUNDINGS, YOUR APPEARANCE, AND YOUR LIFESTYLE UNIQUELY YOUR OWN.

Bunny Williams and her husband, antiques dealer John Rosselli, have created an idyllic life in Falls Village, Connecticut. Expansive cutting gardens and an old barn that has been converted into a guesthouse and space for entertaining surround the 1840 white clapboard Federal-style home she calls Manor House. The couple takes great delight in all aspects of domestic life—entertaining, gardening, and keeping house. "I am always so happy in my conservatory, especially during the day, when the sun is pouring in the skylights, while I care for my plants and daydream." The real beauty of their home lies in the fact that it is truly designed for living.

A master at uncontrived style (both personally and professionally), Bunny also adores dancing, playing charades, doing jigsaw puzzles, and listening to country music and Maria Callas. Bunny's joyful approach to life is clearly reflected in the rooms she creates. She designs homes in which dogs are welcome on the furniture and there is always a place to relax. She first learned the trade and honed her skills working for Parish-Hadley, the iconic American decorating firm known for traditional style, before starting her own business in 1988. "From Mrs. Parish, I learned how to arrange furniture in a room and, from Albert, I learned the importance of scale and proportion." Much like her mentors, the rooms she crafts are grounded in tradition and look as if they have evolved over a long period of time; in fact, many have, including her own. "Time makes a room look even richer," she notes. "I feel the same way about gardens. Once you plant a tree, you want to stick around to see what it's going to look like in thirty years."

**MAKING AN ENTRANCE** An entryway should elicit a sense of excitement and welcome. My favorite welcoming touches include flowers, delectable scents, warm light, a place for coats, and a great mirror. In my home, guests are greeted by rich melon-colored walls and hardwood floors that have been stenciled in a graphic pattern. A white painted Irish table almost always boasts flowers or blooming plants from the greenhouse and a scented candle.

Gracious living isn't merely a buzzword in Bunny's repertoire of expressions; it is a life and style she embodies. She strongly dislikes pretension and believes comfort is of utmost importance. Her cozy library and sunny family room, filled with books, beautifully aged antiques, and softly upholstered chairs, reflect her disposition. It is a house that has been loved and nurtured, not staged with pretty objects. "Mrs. Parish used to say to me, 'you know you can lose a client over a lampshade. You can do the most beautiful work, but if you don't take special care, that is what they are going to remember.'" And while Bunny's style is one of absolute attention to details, she also knows how to keep things relaxed. "I want my style to be creative, playful, and interesting. But I always want it to feel effortless. Style must never be intimidating or forced." Her rooms are not meant to be ends in themselves, but instead a comfortable, sophisticated environment for a rich, full life.

**DECORATIVE DETAILS** Our house is alive because we live in our home. Chairs are always stacked high with books, and tables are covered with magazines. There is a lamp next to every chair and a small drinks table for coffee or wine. We like our guests to help themselves, so a full bar is kept at the ready. Tabletops are never complete without a small flower arrangement.

**CREATURE COMFORTS** My physical well-being is always enhanced by a refreshing walk, several hours in the garden, or a nice long swim. Getting into bed with wonderful sheets guarantees a good night's sleep, which is very important to me. And on my walks, I love to listen to Pandora on my iPhone. As for my emotional well-being, spending time with my friends and family is at the top of my list. I also enjoy working on projects that benefit others such as Trade Secrets, a plant and garden sale held in Sharon, Connecticut, every spring that helps Women's Support Services, or animal rescue efforts.

**A BEAUTIFUL BED** A fabulous bed and comfortable mattress are so important. Our bed was handmade by Charles Beckley. I do not like the new, overly thick mattresses and box springs seen everywhere today. They are of such a terrible proportion. I am partial to the percale sheeting that I purchase from Casa del Bianco in New York and Matouk Linens. On my bed, I use a down blanket purchased from Bed, Bath & Beyond under a quilted blanket cover. It's perfect for year-round use. At the foot of the bed, I like to have a lightweight cover that I can pull over me if I want to nap. In the summer, a light Indian cotton quilt is lovely and in the winter, cashmere makes for a perfect throw.

## FLOWERS AND FRAGRANCES

I am a passionate gardener and grow a lot of shrubs solely for their wonderful fragrances. A few favorites include roses, lilacs, mock orange, and cut apple blossoms. The flowers I most prefer are dahlias, which I grow in colors that look good in the house. I love that they bloom all summer long. As a general rule, I favor flower arrangements that are varying shades of the same color. But sometimes it's fun to mix things up with what you have on hand in the garden. Nothing in the world can replace the wonderful scent of the outdoors. However, the Hedges candle (especially designed for my shop, Treillage) comes in a close second when it perfumes the room with a privet flower hedge aroma.

## ENTERTAINING THOUGHTS

My husband is a wonderful cook and we entertain all the time. Semicasual is our preferred form of gathering friends, and we mostly entertain in our converted barn. There is a huge drinks tray on a French country table behind the sofa so that everyone can help themselves to whatever they want. If the group is larger than fourteen, I will have someone help us serve drinks. We don't do a lot of hors d'oeuvres before dinner— just cheese straws, antipasto, and nuts. Dinner is always a buffet with many dishes. The most important thing is that the host be completely relaxed. Everything should be done ahead of time so you can enjoy the party, too.

# VICENTE WOLF

## STYLE IS THE WAY THAT YOU CHOOSE TO LIVE YOUR LIFE—YOUR VALUES, HOW YOU CARRY YOURSELF, AND HOW YOU INTERACT WITH OTHERS.

Quiet by nature and happy with his own company, Vicente Wolf is a highly complex individual. The Cuban-born designer possesses a fascinating array of traits; he is insightful, curious, shy, opinionated, and witty. Comfortable in his own skin and fully energized by his life at home, few things make him happier than moving photography around his vast apartment, cooking dinner, tending to his plants, and attending the theater (something he does on his own at least three times a week).

His sun-drenched Hell's Kitchen loft plays the perfect supporting role to his multifaceted life. White walls, ceilings, and floors host an amazing collection of photographs, global artifacts, and sixty-five guppies. The small fish inhabit three large water-lily bowls that line a bank of windows facing midtown Manhattan. The water lilies, along with a variety of orchids flourishing in the sunlight, are his constant companions. "They add beauty to my home, they don't speak back, and they bloom all year-round."

Photographs, hundreds by known and unknown artists, casually lean against shelves along the walls. A few by Richard Avedon and Damien Hirst are in the mix. An accomplished photographer himself, he casually remarks, "My collection is displayed in a haphazard way." He never hangs photos and prefers to keep them in a regular rotation. He moves them around as he sees fit. No doubt the unceremoniously displayed photos, sitting atop mismatched chairs, would look "haphazard" in less caring and capable hands.

An avid traveler, who firmly believes travel equals growth, Vicente is always on the hunt for beautiful and interesting

**DECORATIVE DETAILS** I definitely believe in the adage "mix don't match." I gravitate toward the timeless appeal of antiques, the edgy beauty of contemporary design, and touches of exoticism. I like to use furniture and decor to create different balances without being symmetrical. I want objects to neutralize each other, stand out for their beauty, and produce calmness. It's like a dinner party; you don't seat a talkative person next to another talkative person. Each one fills in the gaps. You don't want too much of the same personality side by side.

finds. Ethiopia, Madagascar, Bhutan, Papua New Guinea, Morocco, and Tunisia are just a few of the places that have lured him away from home. Over the years, many collected items have crossed the globe while finding their way to Manhattan. However, each and every decorative object must first have "meaning" and "personality" before making the trek. Don't mistake the designer for a collector. Caretaker is how he describes himself. "All of these objects," he begins, looking around the room, "they will be here forever. I will not. I am just their caretaker until I can pass them on to other people." And while some of his treasures instantly find a home, others leave as fast as they come in the door with the knowledge that many will be replaced by the acquisition of new photos. For the man of few words, perhaps still images best convey the story of his life and style better than any other medium.

**MAKING AN ENTRANCE** "Wow" is the first word that comes to mind whenever I walk through my door. Flowers and an overwhelming amount of natural light always welcome me home. From the moment I walk in, I feel a sense of relaxation. The only thing missing from my home is a lack of pretense, and that's just the way I want it.

**FLOWERS AND FRAGRANCES** I hate it when flowers are missing from my home. I prefer different flowers and scents for many reasons, but I always lean toward orchids, gardenias, freesia, hyacinth, tuberoses, and lilies. For bedrooms, I like shades of pink and cream, but I gravitate toward white or yellow flowers for all other rooms.

**ENTERTAINING THOUGHTS** I entertain all year-round and adhere to seasonally appropriate menus. The food and time of year is more important to me than the setting, which is always casual in nature. Usually, it's a home-cooked meal, a small table set for two, a good bottle of wine, and more food than we'll eat. If it's more than four people, I consider very carefully the seating arrangements.

**CREATURE COMFORTS** Lightly starched and pressed sheets, blooming flowers, sunshine, and surprise snacks in the refrigerator are among my favorite things. I need an environment that lacks self-importance—a place where I can unwind, put up my feet, and entertain friends. For creative, spiritual, and emotional reasons, I need and crave travel; it opens my mind to new people and ideas. Few things bother me more than narrow-mindedness.

**A BEAUTIFUL BED** No bedroom is complete without the scent of fresh flowers, light pouring through the windows in the morning, and good company. Sadly, I don't spend much time in bed and therefore I am always happy when I do get into bed at night. I love lightly starched sateen sheets—always in white and changed every other day. For me, perfection is two Euro pillows, four standard pillows, two boudoir pillows, a cashmere blanket, a Beckley mattress, and fresh sheets.

# SCOT MEACHAM WOOD
## STYLISH LIVING IS INTENTIONAL LIVING.

Scot Meacham Wood can stylishly pull off a bright fuchsia pinwale corduroy jacket and velvet Stubbs & Wootton slippers in the same confident and witty manner in which he decorates his home. The San Francisco designer lives in a milieu inspired by his love of all things tartan, Scottish, and English. It's a wonderfully mad amalgam of colors, textures, and patterns spun together to create a cheerful composition. And while his rooms are luxuriously comfortable, with elements that speak to his Anglophilia, the interiors also possess an undeniable all-American charm. His rooms are the sort you would expect to find in a classic country house rather than a 1940s San Francisco apartment.

Drawing upon his Southern upbringing and thirteen years spent working for Ralph Lauren, Scot creates his own vision of continental style. Every corner bears evidence of his passion: a custom-designed tartan and leather headboard, an antique dresser with horn veneer, and a Chinese needlepoint rug with small creatures running around the edges blanketing the floor. Beautiful furnishings abound, while most of the art evokes memories and a sense of humor. A large art wall composed entirely of portraiture boasts a self-portrait of the artist Stephen O'Donnell and photographs by Robert Frank and fashion photographer George Platt Lynes.

Scot clearly embraces tradition, yet he is not afraid to have fun with his home. His strong suit is giving rooms a hint of a familiar style or period without strict interpretation. "My home is in a constant state of movement and is endlessly reimagined." If things need a change, Scot will update a room without hesitation. After a few years of living without a proper dining room or enough space for dinner parties, the compulsive host swapped his large garden-view bedroom for the private living quarters, converting the rear of his apartment into an open space for gathering friends.

**DECORATIVE DETAILS** Treasured artwork, tokens from my travels, beautiful textiles, and the many artifacts collected over the years add up to tell the story of my life. To fully showcase and appreciate everything in my home, I use lots and lots of lighting, all on dimmers. In fact, proper lighting is one of the most important details in any home. Layers and layers of lighting create a beautiful, interesting, and serene space.

A custom-designed ivory linen velvet sofa and a vintage 1940s brass and glass dining table (being used as a sofa table) now anchor the "front room." An eighteenth-century Belgian bookcase plays the role of a china cabinet, holding his "shamefully" large collection of old English china. The first set of his beloved dishes was purchased in a small San Francisco antiques shop. It was love at first sight, but it took the designer more than an hour to make the purchase. "I knew full well that if I brought those beauties home it would become an unending obsession." Fifteen years and twenty-four place settings later, Scot was correct in his assessment. Today, he continues his quest for tartan-inspired tableware, freely blending new and vintage pieces, always respectful of good design and fine craftsmanship.

**MAKING AN ENTRANCE** The organizational needs of the space are of course important (a place to keep keys and mail, a mirror for that last look before heading out into the world, and maybe a small chair for taking off shoes). But equally important are the emotional components of the entry. Your entry hall is your portal to the world. It is the dividing line between your private life and your public persona. I love seeing something that makes me happy the moment I come home. Usually, it's one of my beloved pieces of artwork.

**FLOWERS AND FRAGRANCES** Fragrances are particularly challenging for me, as I don't have a sense of smell. Out of a need for consistency, I use lavender, fig, and citrus. I am a classicist when it comes to flowers, always opting for bloodred or ivory 'Avalanche' roses. Because there's often a great deal of visual stimulation in my home, I prefer flowers that add only one note to the room. To make a real statement, one huge arrangement of six dozen to eight dozen roses works perfectly.

**A BEAUTIFUL BED** Four sleeping pillows, a down duvet, a feather mattress pad, and several sets of beautiful white bed linens complete my bedding wardrobe. A few years ago I began investing in high-quality percale sheets (Polo White Label, Sferra, D. Porthault). I would like to say that my sheets are always freshly ironed, but it's simply not the case. I treat my house incredibly well, as it does me, but I'm not a slave to it. Sometimes the easiest route is the best one.

**ENTERTAINING THOUGHTS** I have two very distinct and different ways of thinking about entertaining. Christmas is my favorite holiday and my yearly holiday cocktail party is one of my most anticipated events on the calendar; sometimes it can be a year in the planning. Every December the house is at its peak of fabulousness. Conversely, I really love last-minute gatherings, the kind with practically no forethought or planning—it's just great friends, a simple dinner, and maybe a movie.

OUSES OF ENGLAND & WALES
OMERY-MASSINGBERD  CHRISTOPHER SIMON SYKES

OUSES OF SCOTLAND
MASSINGBERD ~ CHRISTOPHER SIMON SYKES

OUSES OF IRELA

# ACKNOWLEDGMENTS

Abounding thanks and gratitude to the gifted designers featured in the pages of *Designers at Home*. I am so grateful for and indebted to each and every one of you. Thank you for sharing your personal thoughts on stylish living. I appreciate not only your beautiful images but also your willingness to open your homes. Sincere appreciation to the photographers who skillfully captured each designer's unique style, and to Gerardo Jaconelli who beautifully captured my workspace. I love our banter.

To my editor, Sandy Gilbert Freidus, you never cease to amaze me. I am so lucky to have worked with you on this book (hopefully the first of many). Thank you for never accepting less than my best efforts and making the whole process enjoyable. You are a great friend. To the exceptionally talented art director, Doug Turshen, and his brilliant designers, Steve Turner and David Huang, thank you for presenting my ideas in such a clear fashion. To everyone at Rizzoli, you are without question extraordinary. A special thank-you to Charles Miers, Nicki Clendening, Jessica Napp, and Pam Sommers. And thanks as well to the rest of the skilled book team: Maria Pia Gramaglia for production management, Hilary Ney and Elizabeth Smith for improving my prose, and Rachel Selekman for proofreading.

A profuse thank-you to Martha Stewart for your willingness to contribute such a thoughtful foreword. You have been a distant mentor for more than twenty years; I have garnered much from your advice and expertise.

Chris, you have been my anchor through every phase of this project and have encouraged me for more than twenty-four years. I appreciate your support and the many home-cooked meals these past few months. We've come a long way since Mrs. Schroyer's high school English class. To my son, Mason, you are without a doubt my biggest supporter and the love of my life. You are the reason I strive to be the best I can—never perfect, but just a little better.

I am fortunate that I was encouraged as a child to dream big. Thank you, Mom, for always telling me, "If you can imagine it, you can achieve it." Abundant gratitude goes to my father who responded to many out-of-the-blue requests for feedback. Michelle, Marilyn, and Tiffany, you are great sisters. Kendel, I am blessed to have a sister-in-law who adores design as well. Finally, to my adorable nieces and nephews, Tyler, Denver, Presley, Pierce, Jordon, Emma, Ella, and Preston, for allowing me to see life through your wondrous eyes.

To my incredible friends who have encouraged my many endeavors: my kindred spirit, dear friend, and sounding board Malcolm James Kutner—brainstorming this book while having lunch at La Fondita in Amagansett seems like ages ago; Bradley Clifford, you inspire me—I adore you; my surrogate sister, Jennifer Taylor Jameson, for always cheering from the sidelines—time and distance will never separate us; Scot Mecham Wood, I adore your fun photos and thoughtful emails; and hosts extraordinaire Michael Devine and Thomas Burak—Thanksgiving in your divine New York City apartment remains a favorite memory. Tammy Connor, I miss you and wish you were closer. My glamorous Glasgow girlfriends, Sara Quinn,

Carmen Reid, and Mairi Mallon, thank you for your camaraderie and inspiring style. And Patricia van Essche, you are a most talented artist. Each day your *All the Best* illustration makes me smile.

I have encountered countless incredible individuals and bloggers since launching *All the Best Blog*. Regrettably, I could never name you all, but I would like to acknowledge some of you here: Mary Aarons, Kim Bachmann, Stacey Bewkes, Becky Birdwell, Simon and Nadine Blake, Elizabeth Blitzer, Jennifer Boles, Sarah Boyd, Kelly Cairns, Leslie Carothers, Alisa Carroll, Dana-Christine Colla, Paloma Contreras, Kelley McCarter Copeland, Suysel dePedro Cunningham, Barbara Elder, Daniel de la Falaise, Lori Dennis, Sophie Donelson, Amy Beth Cupp Dragoo, Gwen Driscoll, Phillip Erdoes, Ann Feldstein, Brian Ferrick, Miguel Flores-Vianna, Anne Maxwell Foster, Penelope Francis, Amanda Frank, Pierre Frey, Shay Geyer, Shani Gilchrist, Lisa Borgnes Giramonti, Keith Granet, Toma Clark Haines, Michael Harold, David Harris, Jane Scott Hodges, Bob Hodgson, Paul Hooker, Kim Huebner, Amanda Jaron, Meg and Christos Joannides, Andrew Joseph, Claudia Farias Kalur, Karen Kreitsek, Christian Leone, Veronica Macasaet, Bethanne Matari, Julia Noran Johnston, Christina Juarez, Rita Konig, Stacy Kunstel, Kate Kutner, Amy Lagae, Amy Lee Lambert, Cassandra LaValle, Marisa Marcantonio, Christian May, Nikki Maxwell, Scott McBee, Kristen McGinnis, Tori Mellot, Tish Mills, Richard Morales, Melissa and Chappy Morris, Erik Perez, Quinn Peeper, Alison Gelb Pincus, Frank Ponterio, Jennifer Powell, Lulu Powers, Jessica Gordon Ryan, Jill Seidner, Rebecca Sherman, Susan Sjölund, Becky Smith, Hollis Smith, Susanna Salk, Peter Sallick, Carolyn Sollis, Anna Spiro, Hugh St. Clair, Andrea Stanford, Tamara Matthews Stephenson, Aaron Stewart, Erik Svensson, Cheminne Taylor-Smith, Maybelline Te, Meg Touborg, Alexis Traina, Freddy Victoria, Brooke Carter Wallace, and Kimberly Schlegel Whitman.

To the following editors and publishers, who have been supportive of me and my blog: Michelle Adams, Parker Bowie, Orli Ben-Dor, Michael Boodro, Jenny Bradley, Beth Brenner, Dara Caponigro, Giulio Capua, D. J. Carey, Diane Carroll, Kerstin Czarra, Stephen Drucker, Carolyn Englefield, Crystal Gentilello, Wendy Goodman, Kyle Hoepner, Barbara King, Ann Maine, Mitch Owens, Paulette Pearson, Amy Preiser, Sabine Rothman, Margaret Russell, Mayer Rus, Anne Sage, Debra Shiver, Clinton Smith, Doretta Sperduto, Jillian St. Charles, Abby Tabak, Matthew Talomie, and Newell Turner. A special thank-you to David Patrick Columbia, the founder and editor of *New York Social Diary*, who inspired me to start blogging. Our lunches at Michael's are always memorable.

Last but certainly not least, an indisputable thank-you to everyone who reads *All the Best*. Your emails and comments always brighten my day. Without your devotion, *Designers at Home* would not exist. So many remarkable persons have motivated me; I can only beg forgiveness of those whose names I have failed to mention.

# PHOTOGRAPHY CREDITS